ABSOLUTE POWER

How the Unitary Executive Theory
Is Undermining the Constitution

John P. MacKenzie

A CENTURY FOUNDATION REPORT

2008 • THE CENTURY FOUNDATION PRESS • NEW YORK

The Century Foundation sponsors and supervises timely analyses of economic policy, foreign affairs, and domestic political issues. Not-for-profit and nonpartisan, it was founded in 1919 and endowed by Edward A. Filene.

LIBRARY OF CONGRESS CATALOGING-IN-PUBLICATION DATA

MacKenzie, John P.
  Absolute power: how the unitary executive theory is undermining the constitution / John P. MacKenzie.
     p. cm.
  Includes bibliographical references and index.
  ISBN 978-0-87078-511-5 (alk. paper)
  1. Executive power--United States. 2. War and emergency powers--United States. 3. Presidents--United States. 4. Constitutional law--United States. I. Title.

KF5050.M33 2007
342.73'06--dc22

                                                                    2007043592

FOREWORD

Over the years, the argument about just what the balance of power should be among the branches of the United States government has served the nation well. It has checked overreach by presidents, courts, and Congress alike. And, it has provided a creative mechanism for the evolution of our government, from one that was well-suited to a largely agrarian society that had yet to experience the industrial revolution, to one that could manage the global and domestic affairs of a modern super state. From time to time, particular challenges—the Civil War, the Great Depression, World War II—have led to a more rough and tumble sorting out of where power should reside and how it should be exercised. Therefore, perhaps it should be no surprise that these matters have returned to center stage in the aftermath of the shock and confusion following the terrorist attacks on September 11, 2001. Those events changed many things and created new concerns, but few predicted that a significant consequence might be the justification and opportunity for a small group to pursue fundamental alterations in the American form of government.

Clearly, along with the horror and pain, there were opportunities for new directions in American policy. Our leaders, for example, might have seized the moment of international empathy for America to forge a grand global coalition against terrorism and its causes. They might have channeled the strong bipartisan support for the president into an era of good feeling, marked by post-partisanship and a government of national unity.

Instead, on many fronts, the Bush administration moved aggressively, branding even those who simply asked for more time and discussion before taking action as dangerous to the nation's security and welfare. The obvious example of this approach was the invasion and occupation of Iraq. But the extraordinary arrests and detentions of suspected terrorists both abroad and at home—and the alarming interrogation techniques employed—all contribute to the record of an administration that believes it makes its own rules, governing as the "decider" without the "inconvenience" of congressional oversight, due process, or bipartisan bargaining.

With regard to advocates of the unitary executive, it is hard not to conclude that terrorism became the reason and excuse to implement their far-reaching dreams of a powerful presidency and a radical agenda. They set out to change the way American government functions on matters small and large.

Revolutions are not always violent, and sometimes do not even make the headlines. But make no mistake, a quiet and intentional revolution has been under way in Washington for the past seven years. Sunshine—in the sense of greater understanding and attention—is clearly needed to bring this revolution to the attention of the American people. We need a more vigorous debate and a more serious comprehension of what is at stake. We are particularly glad, therefore that the author of *Absolute Power*, John MacKenzie, agreed to prepare this report for us.

MacKenzie's long history of work in this area has established him as an astute observer of the ebb and flow of power among the three branches of government. He spent twenty-one years as a reporter for the *Washington Post*, covering the Supreme Court for half that time, and then spent two decades as a *New York Times* editorial writer. He has been a visiting professor of law and a visiting scholar at NYU School of Law, and is the author of *The Appearance of Justice* (Scribners, 1974), which concerns the ethical lapses of judges and justices.

In *Absolute Power*, MacKenzie reviews the key actions that have defined the administration's approach to presidential power, including its attitude toward torture, accountability, war making, eavesdropping, transparency, secrecy, detentions, and habeas corpus, to mention just a few of the topics examined. He explores the implications of the administration's novel approach to presidential bill-signing, in which signing statements interpreting the new statute are asserted to have the force and relevance at least equal and perhaps superior to the record of congressional intent. He points out that Bush has issued more signing statements than all other presidents combined, signaling that he will not enforce all or part of more than seven hundred laws. Those who agreed with the legal reasoning behind the decision in *Bush* v. *Gore*—fear of casting a cloud over the legitimacy of a presidential election—should surely be concerned over recent presidential behavior and signing statements that shake our bedrock assumption that the job of the executive is to see that the laws are faithfully executed.

Like MacKenzie, The Century Foundation also has kept a watchful eye on governmental power. Our recent publications in this area include two volumes of essays examining the erosion of civil liberties after September 11: *Liberty under Attack: Reclaiming Our Freedoms in an Age of Terror* (Public Affairs, 2007) and *The War on Our Freedoms: Civil Liberties in an Age of Terrorism* (Public Affairs, 2003). We also commissioned two books by Stephen J. Schulhofer looking specifically at the effect of the USA PATRIOT Act: *Rethinking the Patriot Act: Keeping America Safe and Free* (Century Foundation Press, 2005) and *The Enemy Within: Intelligence Gathering, Law Enforcement, and Civil Liberties in the Wake of September 11* (Century Foundation Press, 2002). The foundation also has supported work that has detailed the impact of a unitary executive on our foreign policy, such as *Power and Superpower: Global Leadership and Exceptionalism in the 21ˢᵗ Century*, a volume of essays looking at recent perils in American foreign policy.

The obscure legal musings about the implementation of the unitary executive theory began as no more than a cloud "no bigger than a man's hand." Over the past twenty years, the theory has grown to become a strong influence in the halls of power in Washington. The approach and all its effects are only dimly understood by even the most attentive and educated members of the public. In making these developments clear to a wide audience, John MacKenzie is serving a critical and lasting public purpose. On behalf of the Trustees of The Century Foundation, I commend him for this important addition to our understanding of what is at stake in the struggle to prevent runaway executive power.

RICHARD C. LEONE, *President*
THE CENTURY FOUNDATION
December 2007

CONTENTS

Foreword by *Richard C. Leone*   v

1. Introduction   1

2. The Framers   5

3. Jackson, Lincoln, Johnson, Roosevelt, Truman   13

4. The Presidentialists, Domestic   17

5. The Presidentialists, Domestic and Global   31

6. The Presidentialists, Global   35

7. The Will and Pleasure of the President   43

8. Signing Statements   49

9. Theory and Consequence   55

Notes   63

Index   73

About the Author   79

1

INTRODUCTION

The unitary executive theory of national government power holds that the president, given "the executive power" under the Constitution, has virtually all of that power, unchecked by Congress or the courts, especially in critical realms of authority.

Many—not all—of the theory's truest, highest placed believers go further, finding the president endowed with inherent authority beyond conventional bounds for war-waging, national security, and foreign affairs. This is an assertion of absolute power for one of the government's three branches, the executive.

Claiming historical roots, adherents to the theory regard the executive as the branch most important, powerful, and impervious to intrusion of the other two. For those Americans who think of their government as one of shared rather than hoarded powers, this theory reaches a radical, unilateralist extreme.

It could be called the legal philosophy of President George W. Bush, who has invoked it literally hundreds of times, urged by "unitarian" lawyers who proliferate in his Justice Department and White House, encouraged by right-wing think tanks and legal societies, and all orchestrated and executed by Vice President Dick Cheney. The philosophy has driven the administration's boldest claims of the right to stretch or ignore treaties and laws against torture in the "war on terror" and of the power to eavesdrop on the communications of Americans. Believers in the unitary executive even assert that Congress's authorization to use military force, while nice to have, was not constitutionally needed, since Bush had inherent authority to make war in Iraq.

Although the theory is not devoid of all reason, it is weird and ahistorical for a nation that won a revolution against a monarchy and enacted a constitution that rejects a king. Most courts have shunned the theory in legal tests; in fact, two decades ago, the Supreme Court demolished it, 7 to 1, seemingly leaving it for dead and not much mourned except in a long, lone dissent.[1]   However, the theory need not be valid or even alive to be a durable and continuing threat to constitutional balance; witness the speeches by Judge (later Justice) Samuel A. Alito, Jr., seeking to revive it despite the Supreme Court's hostile judgment.[2] And today's Supreme Court harbors three, perhaps four justices who subscribe to it in some measure.

Even if the high court never ratifies the theory, in practice Congress has behaved recently as though the executive had all the powers it claimed. Republicans in Congress have supported President Bush overwhelmingly on the power issues, except for a handful of ineffectual mavericks concerned about the institutional consequences. For example, the Democratic Congress quickened somewhat since the 2006 elections, yet caved in at the president's 2007 request to reduce court involvement over wiretapping in terror-related cases. The increased potency of the presidency may remain no matter who succeeds Bush, since leaders often are reluctant to yield power, however it may have been derived.

In fairness and clarity, presidents of course have always tried to project executive power, usually at the expense of the other branches, and not every claim of predominance has been a unitary extreme.The other branches also have pushed their own envelopes over time. But the fervor and stubborn drive of today's unitarians pale many contests of the past.

For a doctrine of such consequence to lie below the surface of the news is surprising. Yet thousands of pages of learned scholarship, legal memoranda, presidential pronouncements, even Supreme Court opinions have explored the theory, until recently to little public notice.

Bringing the story of the unitary executive into the light of day is essential if we are to bring the nation's governance back into balance. The account in these pages attempts to distill the theorizing, starting with a narrative of its origins. Briefly, it will canvass the historical debate and its consequence first in the Reagan administration. It was during this time that the theory germinated as an argument, in hindsight a relatively modest one, over the powers that the executive branch is obliged to share with the agencies that govern so much of the modern administrative state.

The narrative then will try to capture the moments after September 11, 2001, when the theory was expanded to embrace the grand claims of unilateral power in the Bush administration's terror war. By no means confined to debating circles, the theorists at the Justice Department, Pentagon, and White House starkly applied their power principles to justify torture, at least what most Americans would think of as torture, of terror war detainees. It will then explore how the Supreme Court applied some legal norms to the questions of presidential behavior and told the executive, over a dissent that cited the unitary concept, to share power by obtaining the consent of Congress, and how Congress, vowing never to consent to an imperial presidency, consented when asked.

The battle for and over presidential power has become increasingly strident, not only in the terror war, but also in other venues of law and policy. The unitary executive has fueled volumes of presidential signing statements announcing the right to ignore, or nullify by interpretation, laws passed by Congress—and signed by the president himself. The theory appears to have helped feed the recent controversial firing of United States attorneys.

It may prove significant that not every unitarian is a radical extremist of the stripe that produced the Bush administration torture memoranda. Uncounted devotees, and one of the movement's most prominent leaders, cling to the more modest, arcane domestic variety of the theory that merely longs to roll back features of the administrative state wrought by the New Deal.

Whether in its radical form or more moderate incarnation, this theory is no basis for running a government, but it has been used continually to drive and to attempt to rationalize many executive branch policies and practices over the past two decades. Although lawyers understand it best, the theory nourishes a political world view, a president-oriented one that helps justify unilateral actions around the globe and slights the role of consultation and power-sharing abroad. President Bush is no theoretician, but the theory drives his administration nevertheless, and its unilateralism comfortably supports his view of himself as the domestic and global "decider." Still, the theory, when examined, is historically baseless.

What is to be done? Aside from a change in executive personnel and policy, the answer must lie in a rejuvenated, reformed Congress—which despite changing party control has shown little aspiration or strength for revival or reform. Congress must correct the excesses committed under the umbrella of a unitary executive and prevent new ones, for the sake of the institutions that guard the Constitution, regardless of the political party in control of Congress or the White House. Even if a major shift in national outlook takes place, the theory in question cannot be counted upon to die but rather, if only because of the unsinkable zeal of its believers, it may remain at the fringes of American life indefinitely. So the unitary executive needs to be understood and resisted with a firmer grasp of the nation's formative ideals and best character.

2

THE FRAMERS

Ask a true unitarian where the unitary executive came from, and a likely answer will be "Alexander Hamilton." Expanding the question to mean the unitary executive as an operating doctrine, an ideology, a litigating tenet, a unifying principle, a slogan, an icon, a rallying cry—whatever it is the Bush administration has been pushing—and the answer will shift to "Oh, you must mean somewhere in the Justice Department during the second Reagan Administration."

Hamilton is indeed a favorite source of the concept, though not the term, which had yet to be coined. That happened somewhere within the Justice Department after Edwin Meese III moved from the White House, where he had been counselor to President Reagan, to become attorney general in 1985. The preceding two centuries provided numerous contests over executive power. They set the stage for the Bush administration's deep, wide claims—deep into the bureaucracy to gain control, then wide in the world of expansive "inherent" powers of war and foreign affairs.

Without doubt, the struggles over power among the branches are authentic, even primal, built into the Constitution's separation of powers, checks and balances, and grants and limitations on power. Just as ferocious in their way are the arguments by some scholars that the strong, unitary executive is a matter of the original intent of the Constitution's framers.

The case for the unitary executive consumes hundreds of heavily footnoted books and law review pages. Among the complex arguments, two themes recur among many. One is "energy in the executive," comprising strong general and enumerated, and sometimes "inherent," powers. The other is a defense to any control by Congress based on constitutional checks and balances. Both arguments claim attention, but each fails on examination.

The term *unitary* does not surface in and around the 1787 constitutional convention. Some framers, Hamilton especially, spoke of "unity"—not to broaden the sweep of executive power but rather to describe the framers' early choice of a single-person executive as opposed to some multi-headed committee or council. On James Madison's initiative, and with relative ease, the convention chose to design an executive headed by a single individual, whatever his relationship to the rest of government might prove to be. Under the discredited Articles of Confederation, there was no separate executive at all, just a congress of thirteen state delegations. In other words, it was a thirteen-part legislature—overseen by a pseudo-manager—whose members often bound themselves to act unanimously, if at all, and were forced to beg their constituent states for resources and cooperation. It was a perfect recipe for gridlock.

The founding generations had been averse to executive power in the person of a king, but the American answer was not to have a headless state. The Declaration of Independence indicted George III for high-handed disregard for the rights of Englishmen in North America. The Constitution's creators were never less hostile to the British Crown, but they came to realize that the new nation needed a chief executive to administer more efficiently the affairs of the national government and an executive that did not have to implore the states for revenue and cooperation.

As they deliberated, the framers did have in their midst at least one closet royalist—Hamilton. In a six-hour speech to the Philadelphia convention on one antic afternoon in 1787, Hamilton advocated a monarch elected for life. Then he lurched to suggest an even stronger regression to the British system: "He ought to be hereditary and to have so much power that it will not be his interest to risk much to acquire more." Nobody seconded that notion, and a biographer records that "he never again uttered a kind word for monarchy." Indeed, despite his quarrels with the new Constitution, Hamilton—most energetically—promoted it. Madison, the Constitution's preeminent father, said of him, "No man's ideas were more remote from the plan [in the proposed Constitution] than his were known to be," yet he readily joined Hamilton's monumental project, *The Federalist*. [1]

So it is somewhat natural that the unitarians look most fervently to Hamilton as a framer who embraced a strong, vigorous presidency. "Energy in the Executive," he wrote in *The Federalist,* "is the leading character in the definition of good government."[2] This is the bedrock of the historical argument for a unitary executive branch, the modern pitch for the strongest kind of executive, and is perhaps the strongest foundation for the unitary executive.[3] What did Hamilton mean by this?

Hamilton wrote fifty-two of the eighty-five papers of *The Federalist,* serial newspaper articles urging New Yorkers to ratify the new Constitution, and guides ever since to interpretation or argument over the document. Madison wrote twenty-eight of them, and John Jay, the future governor of New York, ambassador, and chief justice of the United States, wrote five.

Scour *The Federalist* for references to energy and unity. While the writers all deplored the lack of energy and ridiculed the "plurality" of the Confederation's structure of executive power, the energetic executive everywhere connotes unity only in the sense of a single manager, as opposed to plural managers. *The Federalist* No. 70, written by Hamilton and one of the essays most often saluted by unitarians, argues, "That unity is conducive to energy will not be disputed. Decision, activity, secrecy and dispatch will generally characterize the proceedings of one man in a much more eminent degree than the proceedings of any greater number." That unity "may be destroyed in two ways," Hamilton said. One was to load up the executive with two or more equally powerful magistrates; the other was to encumber a single executive with a council of helpful advisers.

The need for a strong, nimble executive, Hamilton made clear on the same day, March 18, 1788, in *The Federalist* No. 71, is to be able to stand up to an inevitably self-aggrandizing Congress. "The tendency of the legislative authority to absorb every other," he said, was plain from the experience of other countries.

Madison agreed. "Energy in government is essential," he argued in *The Federalist* No. 37, both for national security and "that prompt and salutary execution of the laws which enter into the very definition of good government." He concluded, "energy in government requires not only a certain duration of power," the presidential term of office, "but the execution of it by a single hand."

Madison did not merely concede the point, he proclaimed it. The accumulation of legislative, executive, and judicial powers in one part of government "may justly be pronounced the very definition of tyranny."[4] For that much of his argument he, too, is adopted by unitarians. But the unitarians too often stop with that challenging statement, whereas to appreciate Madison's larger point demands both patience and a sense of theater.

The imposing French philosopher Montesquieu heavily influenced civic thinkers of his day with his championship of separation of powers. Many state constitutions of the Confederation had already paid homage to the principle, most starkly that of Massachusetts:

> In the government of this Commonwealth, the legislative department shall never exercise the executive and judicial powers, or either of them: The executive shall never exercise the legislative and judicial powers, or either of them: The judicial shall never exercise the legislative and executive powers, or either of them: to the end it may be a government of laws and not of men.

Enter Madison again in *The Federalist* No. 47. First, a deep bow to the French baron:

> The oracle who is always consulted and cited on this subject is the celebrated Montesquieu. If he be not the author of this invaluable precept in the science of politics, he has the merit at least of displaying and recommending it most effectually to the attention of mankind. Let us endeavor, in the first place, to ascertain his meaning on this point.

Montesquieu did not mean there should be no inter-branch control at all, Madison argued, only "that where the whole power of one department is exercised by the same hands which possess the whole power of another department, the fundamental principles of a free constitution are subverted." Continuing, he writes:

> If we look into the constitutions of the several States, we find that, notwithstanding the emphatical and, in some instances, the unquali- fied terms in which this axiom has been laid down, there is not a single instance in which the several departments of power have been kept absolutely separate and distinct.

No full monty this, but rather a nuanced view that informs several present-day Supreme Court opinions. Surveying all thirteen states, Madison found blended as well as separated powers, no less in rigid, dogmatic Massachusetts than elsewhere:

> This declaration [in the Massachusetts constitution] corresponds precisely with the doctrine of Montesquieu, as it has been explained, and is not in a single point violated by the plan of the convention. It goes no farther than to prohibit any one of the entire departments from exercising the powers of another department. In the very Constitution to which it is prefixed, a partial mixture of powers has been admitted. The executive magistrate has a qualified negative on the legislative body, and the Senate, which is a part of the legislature, is a court of impeachment for members both of the executive and judiciary departments. The members of the judiciary department, again, are appointable by the executive department, and removable by the same authority on the address of the two legislative branches. Lastly, a number of the officers of government are annually appointed by the legislative department.

So much, for now, about the meaning and role of energy in our constitutional framework, and for how strictly the framers separated the powers, or meant to do so. Whatever Constitution the states ratified, the very first Congress set quickly to interpreting, notably in what historians call "The Decision of 1789."

The first Congress that convened after ratification often has been anointed with having special qualities of understanding the Constitution. Many of those who met in Philadelphia had been members of the constitutional convention. They promptly made good on the pledge to submit a list of amendments—the Bill of Rights—to the states. They also grappled with a question left open at Philadelphia, one that plagued the unitary executive debate two centuries later. The question was whether the president's power to appoint officers subject to Senate confirmation entitled the president to remove those same officers unilaterally, without Senate approval.

In establishing the departments of War, Foreign Affairs, and Treasury, the first Congress considered Madison's proposal to make clear that each Senate-confirmed secretary was "removable by the President."[5] The legislators labored exquisitely over whether to make a declarative statement about where that power lay, or to continue to leave it unspoken. Madison argued, as did many presidential supporters over the generations, that at least at the level of secretary, the unaided or unencumbered removal power was necessary if the president was to be held to his duty to "take care that the laws be faithfully executed." He also maintained that the nature of the office being created should guide Congress in determining how much to participate in the removal process, an argument that colored congressional decisions about whether to limit a president's removal when it comes to some officers, for example, to "good cause."

As for these consequential offices, Congress ultimately did not legislate a role for itself, nor did it accept Madison's forthright direction of the president's unilateral power. Instead, it opted for subtle indirection. The clerk of each department was authorized to hold custody of department records whenever the department's top officer "shall be removed from office by the President of the United States." Chief Justice William Howard Taft, noting the special perspective of the first Congress, ruled in 1926 that this "Decision of 1789" amounted to more than a legislative choice. The former president found it the best interpretation of the Constitution's recognition of this executive power. He said the president could fire, for no reason, not only his cabinet officers but also jobholders as lowly as second-class postmaster.

To save some cranial strain, let us skip ahead to our own day: Taft is right that Congress must allow the president to fire his high, Senate-confirmed officers unilaterally. However, he is wrong that the chief executive also can fire many of the lowest functionaries. In designing and shaping the executive departments in legislation, Congress may lay down special requirements, such as identifying misconduct in office, for the firing of lower-level officials. There is a still unsettled gray area between high and low, because of the infinite variety of ranks, offices, agencies, and functions.

So, this is how things stood. We had the Constitution and the precedents set by the First Congress.

Article I bestows "all the legislative powers herein granted" upon Congress, including the power to declare war, to maintain and set rules for the military and the treatment of prisoners captured "on land and water," to regulate interstate and foreign commerce, to enact laws necessary and proper for executing its powers, to impeach and remove all officers, and, for the Senate, to confirm or reject nominees for the judiciary and executive officers.

Article II vests "the executive power" in the president and identifies or grants some specified authority—or duty—to nominate officers and judges subject to Senate confirmation, to negotiate treaties subject to Senate ratification, to veto bills subject to congressional override, to command the military, and "to take care that the laws be faithfully executed."

Article III vests "the judicial power" in one Supreme Court and the congressionally created lower judiciary, and grants tenure for good behavior with undiminished compensation.

As Justice Potter Stewart once said, the Constitution "establishes the contest, not its resolution."[6] Indeed, as history has moved on, members of the executive, the legislature, and the judiciary have tested the limits of their offices. A fairly rapid survey of some skirmishes among the branches will give an idea of the nature of the contests that are important to the unitarians.

3

JACKSON, LINCOLN, JOHNSON, ROOSEVELT, TRUMAN

The annals of contested presidential power fill volumes. A few episodes in particular serve to exhibit the flavor of the struggle and perhaps provide precedents for present-day battles.

"Well, John Marshall has made his decision, now let him enforce it." Whether Andrew Jackson made that precise statement regarding Chief Justice Marshall or not, he most dramatically acted it out. Jackson, the most thunderous claimant to the Constitution's duty to "take care that the laws be faithfully executed," was faithless to his duty to execute the Cherokee treaty,[1] upheld by the Supreme Court, that vindicated native rights to land in Georgia.

With equal clamor, Jackson claimed that the enforcement duty contained in Article II fully authorized his removal of two Treasury secretaries so that he could appoint one that would obey his command to sink the Second Bank of the United States. How else to faithfully execute the laws if you cannot remove officers who refuse to do it your way?[2]

Military force, backing up rapacious Georgians, upheld Jackson's decision to ignore the Supreme Court, defy the Cherokee treaty, and stand firm against the Native Americans, but history judges him harshly. As to the power to remove high-ranking officers without hindrance by Congress, legal history has vindicated Jackson's power, though not necessarily his tact or economic judgment. A jealous Senate, futilely striving to keep the Second Bank afloat, censured the president as a usurper but later expunged that judgment.

Abraham Lincoln famously was discreet but not shy about exercising and expanding his executive authority during the Civil War. Responding swiftly to advancing Confederate troops, he unilaterally and selectively ordered his generals to suspend the writ of habeas corpus for captured citizens identified as threats to Union troop movements. History tends to acquit Lincoln of impropriety if only because he informed Congress, which had been away, of his emergency action and obtained Congress's retroactive approval. Before that, as a candidate, he had raised the question of interpreting the Constitution contrary to the Supreme Court's decision in *Dred Scott v. Sandford*. In office, he rendered the nation's stand on the slavery issue with the Emancipation Proclamation, unilaterally invoking war powers.[3]

Andrew Johnson's role in the history of presidential power somewhat parallels Jackson's, though in drastically more stressful circumstances, which produced his impeachment. Deeply unpopular with the postwar Congress, he fired his inherited secretary of war in defiance of the Tenure of Office Act and other laws designed to constrain his removal powers. The House of Representatives impeached him, and the Senate tried him, falling one vote short of the necessary two-thirds majority to convict. As with Jackson, history has vindicated Johnson's removal authority for officers of secretarial rank, though not his leadership or political wisdom.[4]

By the time the issue of the president's unilateral removal power landed squarely in the Supreme Court, the statutory setting had shifted several times, partly from the interplay of civil service reform and spoils politics. Woodrow Wilson's firing of an Oregon postmaster named Frank Myers disregarded both the employee's statutory four-year term and a postal law requiring the Senate's advice and consent for removal. The decision in *Myers v. United States*, which went in favor of presidential power, may in retrospect be a peak of prestige for what later advocates would call the unitary executive. The ruling's short life was presaged by dissents from Holmes, Van Devanter, and Brandeis—containing ominous warning that Chief Justice Taft had overstated his case.

Franklin D. Roosevelt's firing of a Federal Trade commissioner brought the issue back to the Supreme Court. Early in his first term he fired a Senate-confirmed Hoover holdover, William E. Humphrey. The grounds were not "inefficiency, neglect of duty or malfeasance in office" as the Federal Trade Commission (FTC) Act required, but simply Roosevelt's view that he and the business-oriented Humphrey could not "go along together" on the commission's regulatory mission. In *Humphrey's Executor* v. *United States*, a unanimous Supreme Court used a few pages to erase much of Taft's wordy opinion delivered only nine years earlier.

Justice Sutherland, a member of the *Myers* majority and no special friend of the FTC's regulatory mission, disavowed the reach of *Myers* so far below policy levels, indicating that while the high political ranks were subject to the president's unilateral dismissal, the members of the independent agencies with their partly judicial, partly lawmaking powers, could be safeguarded from firing other than for cause.[5] Taft also had carved out an exception to the removal power when it came to executive officers with adjudicatory functions.

Four presidential terms later, Harry S. Truman tested his own uncertain powers and lost. In 1952, in the midst of a war in Korea not declared by Congress but denominated a United Nations police action, the president took possession of the nation's strikebound steel industry rather than invoke the stay provisions of the Taft-Hartley Act, which he despised and which had been passed over his veto. He seized the mills, reported to Congress, and waited for ratification. That never arrived, but the steel industry's lawsuit did. In *Youngstown Sheet & Tube Co.* v. *Sawyer,* the Supreme Court held that Truman lacked this authority.[6]

Justice Hugo Black, a Senate alumnus and champion of legislative power, spoke for six justices in the majority, each of whom chimed in with essays of his own. No unitarian could have argued more strenuously than Truman's lawyers for all the powers that could be mined from Article II and "inherent powers" above and beyond the Constitution. They spoke of a dire national defense emergency, but, as Justice Felix Frankfurter noted in a concurrence, "reliance on the powers that flow from declared war has been commendably disclaimed by the Solicitor General." Reaching a bit further, Frankfurter said the country was "not at war, in the only constitutional way in which it can be at war."[7]

Justice Robert Jackson filed his memorable, seminal concurrence in this case,[8] writing more elegantly, "While the Constitution diffuses power the better to secure liberty, it also contemplates that practice will integrate the dispersed powers into a workable government. It enjoins upon its branches separateness but interdependence, autonomy but reciprocity." He offered this "somewhat oversimplified" set of circumstances in which the president's power is asserted or challenged:

1. When the President acts pursuant to an express or implied authorization of Congress, his authority is at its maximum, for it includes all that he possesses in his own right plus all that Congress can delegate.

2. When the President acts in absence of either a congressional grant or denial of authority, he can only rely upon his own independent powers, but there is a zone of twilight in which he and Congress may have concurrent authority, or in which its distribution is uncertain.

3. When the President takes measures incompatible with the expressed or implied will of Congress, his power is at its lowest ebb, for then he can rely only upon his own constitutional powers minus any constitutional powers of Congress over the matter.

Youngstown Sheet & Tube Co. v. *Sawyer* gave the president and the nation a civics lesson and a guide to the legal power balance of government that dominated the constitutional landscape for the half-century that followed and, people may hope, beyond. The Constitution thus interpreted set the stage for the interplay of powers, but not its resolution. That would still be up to Congress and the president, with occasional intervention from the courts.

4

THE PRESIDENTIALISTS, DOMESTIC

The lawyers who gathered under Attorney General Edwin Meese III during Reagan's second term (1985–89) were for the most part collegial team players. They reveled in their freedom to think and strategize to enlarge the power of their popular president, who in turn licensed Meese. Meese empowered them to litigate and lobby to change the legal culture.

Some of these change agents came to call themselves *unitarians*, not of the religious denomination but adherents to the theory of the unitary executive. Another term they applied to themselves, in endless legal tracts, was *presidentialist*, an advocate for recognizing the vastness of presidential power.

As actors joined in the mission to give their president dominion over the immense government bureaucracy, they were far from unique. Every administration takes the reins of power expecting the horses to go, but they find layers of management that resist. Even politicians who sought the White House to rid the nation of regulation must begin by issuing regulations, usually attempts to consolidate power. The White House's Office of Management and Budget is schooled in these reorganization techniques, but the president's team tries to learn how to take over those reins.[1]

Out across Washington, lawyers in the Reagan departments looked to contests with Congress and the judiciary, but all hands found that the power they called executive had been distributed far and wide, usually to agencies that enjoyed some independence from the executive. To some degree these lawyers felt they were heirs of Andrew Jackson, Abraham Lincoln, Andrew Johnson, Franklin D. Roosevelt, and Harry S. Truman, to mention only those presidents we glanced at in the previous chapter. Young but well read, they felt the weight of decades of power loss that began quietly enough with the Interstate Commerce Commission in 1887 and exploded under Roosevelt.

These hardy legal eagles, many fresh from the political minority ranks of major law schools, had the relatively modest goal of defanging the riot of agencies wrought by the New Deal. Later, some of their intellectual cousins would take the power struggle to new realms of war-making.

Collegiality may help explain why none of these legal warriors will claim to have coined the term *unitary executive*. Steven G. Calabresi, cofounder of the Federalist Society and a close Meese assistant, has become perhaps the most widely published advocate of the theory, but he disowns authorship or knowledge of the author of the theory's name.[2] The Federalist Society, starting in 1982 at a handful of law schools, already was providing streams of like-minded law graduates. One of the society's earliest mentors was T. Kenneth Cribb, for many years a sponsor of conservative college campus groups who worked with Meese both at the White House and Justice. In a few short years, the society was neither lacking for funds nor requests to help conservative administrations recruit conservative, motivated, energetic officers.[3]

Reagan's first Justice Department, under William French Smith, his once and future personal lawyer, seemed conservative enough, engaging in ideological and power battles over civil rights and abortion, but the energy that Meese generated was palpable. A trusted Reagan confidant from his California days, Meese realized a life's ambition when his president nominated him for attorney general in 1984. Delayed by an independent counsel investigation of his ethics, he took office a year later, and hit the ground running. His top lawyers met often, and many felt like brothers as they debated constitutional issues over lunch and through the day.

Meese quickly ignited a brainstorming mission, assigning Steven J. Markman, then assistant attorney general for legal policy and now a justice of the Michigan Supreme Court, to produce a dozen research reports on the future of constitutional law. Collectively, these slim paperbacks, though not widely distributed, represented a constitutional agenda within the department. These studies ranged from quarrels with current ways of interpreting statutes,[4] to the future of judicial review,[5] to private property rights.[6] One early blue book took issue with the great Chief Justice John Marshall's broad blessing in 1816 of Congress's power to enact all laws "necessary and proper" for carrying out the mission of government.

That clause, and Marshall's announcement that the judiciary would only very rarely challenge its exercise, soon proved to be one of the main sources of congressional power the courts cited to blow away unitary executive claims.

A burst of Supreme Court cases at first vindicated the Reagan administration's program to slow or halt the scattering of power. The first Reagan administration was on the winning side of a case, initiated by a private party, declaring unconstitutional the so-called legislative veto, an odd inversion of the lawmaking process. In literally hundreds of bills, starting with the Hoover administration, Congress would pass a law giving decisional authority to an agency yet retaining the power to disapprove specific rules or actions. Disapproval could always legitimately come from an act of Congress, but this veto could be exercised by one chamber, one committee, or sometimes a powerful committee chairman. Just about every president has complained about this congressional assumption of executive power yet they all went along with it for the sake of convenience.

Tests of this behavior were elusive until the practice took on a human face, that of one Jagdish Rai Chadha, a Kenyan native whose expired student visa exposed him to deportation. The law authorized the attorney general to block deportations on hardship grounds, subject to the veto of the House or Senate—in reality subject to the rule of a committee chairman clinging to petty power.

In 1983, in *Immigration and Naturalization Service* v. *Chadha*, the Supreme Court struck down this practice as violating the regular constitutional way of legislating. In practical terms the victory meant little—Congress proceeded to pass scores of legislative vetoes and presidents kept complaining and kept on signing, to avoid punishing negotiations with tough committee chairmen. (A survey of presidential signing statements showed that President George Bush registered forty-one objections based on *Chadha* to bills he signed into law from 2001 through August 2007.[9]) Yet the theorists for executive power were encouraged by the ruling, for it showed the Court's willingness to curb Congress. Although the legislative veto itself sometimes served the interests of both Congress and the president, they sought to build on the Congress-curbing features of the decision.

Meese moved right along. In speeches, including a publicized speech to the American Bar Association's House of Delegates in Washington, he accused the Supreme Court of substituting its will for the Constitution's true meaning according to the framers' intent. He criticized the Court's extension of Bill of Rights provisions to the states, saying it rested on an "intellectually shaky foundation . . . and nowhere else has the principle of federalism been dealt so politically violent and constitutionally suspect a blow."[10] He engaged Justices William J. Brennan, Jr., and John Paul Stevens, who fired back rare responses. Stevens replied that Meese had failed to mention that no justice in sixty years had questioned the application of the Bill of Rights to the states under the Fourteenth Amendment. Asked for comment, Terry Eastland, Meese's spokesman, said the involvement of judges in the discussion was welcome.[11] Indeed, the Justice Department got a kick out of getting a rise out of the judges. And more than a kick: recognition. Meese said two decades later, "It was when we spoke up in opposition that suddenly we had a debate, and that gave it more attention. I suspect that if Justce Brennan had not replied, my speech in 1985 would have gone with most American Bar Association speeches into the proceedings never to be heard from again."[12]

From a kernel of accuracy—that executive officials had their own duty to interpret and obey the Constitution—Meese argued that the administration need not abide by a high court ruling in cases to which the United States was not a party. He was right about the executive branch's duty to interpret the Constitution in the first instance, in order to enforce it. (Indeed, former Justice Arthur J. Goldberg and his former law clerk Alan Dershowitz of Harvard Law School argued in 1970 that state governors had the legitimate power to interpret the Eighth Amendment's ban on cruel and unusual punishments as forbidding the death penalty and thus the chief executives should block all executions unilaterally.[13]) But Meese was far out of the mainstream to contend that the Court's constitutional interpretation did not bind him.[14] Meese's rhetoric, though contested at the time, nevertheless served as a theoretical platform for presidents such as George W. Bush to claim that their inherent powers entitled them to withhold enforcement of parts of acts of Congress they had signed.[15]

In this vein, Meese's litigating team tasked a young lawyer named Samuel Alito to research a subject dear to the attorney general's heart.

Meese wanted to publish, as part of the legislative history of bills passed and signed, the president's own remarks at the signing, giving his interpretation of the law. Alito responded enthusiastically, stating that the president's views were every bit as indicative of the law's meaning as those of Congress's expressed in conventional legislative history. He said the publication of "presidential intent" could curb abuses of legislative history and "increase the power of the Executive to shape the law."[16] Courts often resort to the history of legislation—in congressional hearings and floor debates—to clarify ambiguities. The West Publishing Company agreed to include presidential signing statements, which already were public documents, in its compilation of congressional materials frequently consulted by litigators. "Presidential intent" may be interesting but, expressed after Congress has completed its work, it is hardly a substitute for legislative intent, which lawyers and judges study to ascertain the meaning of a legislative act. Partly for that reason, scholars have found no instance where a court found the president's signing remarks decisive or influential in the sense intended, though some courts did mention them.

As aggressive as Meese was on many fronts, his main thrust may have come in a speech to the Federal Bar Association in Detroit in September 1985. Meese raised questions about the constitutionality of the "independent" federal agencies, which he found had eroded presidential power since the New Deal and foiled the president's duty to see that the laws were faithfully executed. Meanwhile, his lawyers were asserting that these agencies, however ancient their pedigrees, might be illegitimate because they violated the principle of the unitary executive.

Meese's public statements, much more than any legal pleadings, haunted the next major Supreme Court case, *Bowsher* v. *Synar*,[17] a challenge initiated by six members of Congress to the Gramm-Rudman-Hollings Act, formally known as the Balanced Budget and Emergency Deficit Control Act of 1985. The law was an elaborate attempt to accomplish budget cuts without political cost to members of Congress. In the center of the law's plan were fiscal calculations to be made by the comptroller general, triggering scheduled percentages of budget reductions. The comptroller, Charles A. Bowsher, an independent-minded public servant, was officially considered an agent of Congress, but his duty under this statute seemed executive in nature. Many would agree that whatever Bowsher's personal probity, the important thing was who could fire him. Congress hired him and only Congress's initiative could cause his removal by passing a joint resolution, albeit one that would be signed by the president or passed over his veto. President Reagan signed the budget bill but complained about the comptroller's role. His lawyers saw a chance to diminish Congress's power to keep fiscal matters on a leash, power they claimed, with some fairness, that the comptroller was exercising at the expense of the executive.

In his Supreme Court brief, Solicitor General Charles Fried, citing Hamilton's *Federalist* No. 70 about the energetic executive, said, "The Framers deliberately settled upon a unitary executive in order to promote a sense of personal responsibility and accountability to the people in the execution of the laws—and thereby to ensure vigorous administration of the laws and protection of the liberty, property, and welfare of the people." That, he argued, precluded assigning an executive task—the politically consequential fiscal calculation—to an officer who owed his job to another branch. In two centuries of Supreme Court history this was the first reference in Court pleadings to the "unitary executive." The term was not signaled to the general public, and functionally it added nothing to the traditional arguments based simply on the separation of powers.

Fried made no reference to the unitary executive term in his oral argument, nor did any justice use it when the case was decided. But the Meese rhetoric, questioning the regulatory agencies with their varied functions and sources of job protection, did echo in the high court's chamber. Although Fried later wrote that he had "combed out of our brief any direct attack on the independent agencies," his opposing counsel contended that his argument was broad enough to undo decades of agency creation. Fried replied that these were "scare tactics." To which Justice Sandra Day O'Connor replied, "Well, Mr. Fried, you certainly scared me."[18]

It would be too much to say, though it often is said, that the staid, ornate courtroom erupted in laughter, but this exchange more than passed for high legal humor. It also may have marked the cresting of Meese's movement and his unitary executive. The Court struck down the law, but Chief Justice Warren Burger's opinion for the Court took pains to point out that no other federal agencies or offices were implicated. As initially disclosed by Bernard Schwartz, a prodigious discoverer of unpublished pre-decision opinions, Burger drafted an initial opinion that might have questioned the agencies, but his colleagues forced him to narrower grounds.[19]

Meese's energy knew no bounds, but his agenda started to falter as the lame duck Reagan term progressed. Republicans lost the Senate in 1986, and with it control of the confirmation of Robert H. Bork to the Supreme Court, which failed by a vote of 58 to 42. The Iran-Contra scandal erupted, the president appeared befuddled, and his team fell under an independent counsel investigation.

Congress buried the administration in ridicule for its Iran-Contra adventures, although, prophetically, Representative Dick Cheney dissented, not merely defending Iran-Contra, but also denouncing Congress for meddling in the realm of presidential "inherent power," a harbinger of the expansive commander-in-chief brand of the unitary executive promoted later in the Bush-Cheney regime. That dissent was a seedbed for a more expansive form of unitary executive theory and practice, as the next chapter will discuss.[20]

As for the more modest form of unitary executive theory, the domestic policy that contested features of administrative agency power, the curtain was about to come down on that aspect of the Meese agenda. Meese attacked the constitutionality of the Independent Counsel Act of 1978, and in 1988 lost in the Supreme Court by a lopsided 7 to 1 in *Morrison v. Olson*. The law itself died a decade later at age 21, not of unconstitutionality but of malnourishment and abuse.

Hated beast of unitarians everywhere, the law grew out of the Saturday Night Massacre of October 1973, when Richard M. Nixon ordered the firing of Archibald Cox, the special prosecutor investigating the president. Cox had been appointed by the attorney general and given broad prosecutorial powers under Justice Department regulations forbidding his removal "except for extraordinary improprieties on his part."[21]

Nixon did not pretend that Cox had been malfeasant, merely that he disobeyed orders in seeking evidence, though it was Nixon who stood accused of his own gross impropriety. Public pressure forced the appointment of a replacement, Leon Jaworsky, whose victory[22] in quest of evidentiary tapes over Nixon's claim of executive privilege drove the president from office. Congress began work on a structure for conflict-of-interest prosecutorial situations. The job security had to come from a statute, not rescindable regulations.

Unitarians objected to any law that interfered with the executive branch's power to prosecute. They said Congress could not mess with the president's "duty to see that the laws be faithfully executed." To insulate the independent counsel from arbitrary White House action, the law called on a rarely used provision in Article II of the Constitution. This provides that, in addition to the appointment of "principal officers" with Senate advice and consent, "the Congress may by law vest the appointment of such inferior officers, as they think proper, in the President alone, in the Courts of Law, or in the Heads of Departments." The law created a special division of the United States Court of Appeals for the District of Columbia to choose independent counsels on application by the attorney general.

The law was complex, with rules and hair triggers aimed at one goal: to prevent the executive branch from prosecuting—and more important, exonerating—its high-ranking officers when credibly implicated in wrongdoing. It was a conflict-of-interest statute, which several presidents and attorneys general contended was unconstitutional because only a prosecutor appointed by the president, and removable by the president or his attorney general, could prosecute the president or his official family.

Many, including Edwin Meese, have studiously ignored one of the major objectives of the law and of the independent or special counsel generally. That objective is not merely to ensure that favored officials do not evade prosecution, but also to exonerate accused officials credibly when appropriate. It was especially unbecoming for Meese, who was twice absolved of criminal liability by a court-appointed independent counsel. On the other hand, to Meese's credit, even as his lawyers attacked the statute, he offered parallel appointments to all independent counsels in addition to their court appointments he was contesting, to avoid any claim of bad faith based on the fact that he and other Reagan officials were being investigated by Lawrence E. Walsh, the independent counsel.

Into this statutory maw stepped Theodore B. Olson, assistant attorney general in charge of the Office of Legal Counsel. He and two other high Justice Department officials became enmeshed in battles with House committees investigating abuses of the Superfund environmental cleanup law. The investigations prompted criminal charges and demands for documents and ultimately a complaint that Olson had withheld documents and truthful information. Meese reluctantly applied to the Court for an independent counsel to investigate Olson, but not before personally exonerating his deputy and college classmate Edward C. Schmults and another assistant attorney general. Schmults said he had provided inaccurate information but that he had intended to correct the record. When Congress next renewed the act it specified that the attorney general may not step in and exonerate in this fashion.

Olson challenged the appointment of the independent counsel, Alexia Morrison, on separation of powers grounds. In the Court of Appeals he had Justice Department support in his attack on the law. The Justice Department's brief used the phrase *unitary executive* a dozen times. The appellate panel, splitting 2 to 1, ruled for Olson and against the law. Judge Laurence H. Silberman's majority opinion, joined by Judge Stephen F. Williams, used the *unitary executive* term half a dozen times. Judge (later Justice) Ruth Bader Ginsburg dissented.[23]

Judge Silberman's use of the term *unitary executive* marked its first use in any federal court opinion. Yet despite its novelty on the judicial scene, the judge insisted on its gravity and application to the case. "Central to the government instituted by the Constitution are the doctrines of separation of powers and a unitary executive," he wrote, "and yet the independent counsel interprets the appointments clause as if those doctrines were nonexistent." It was a somewhat jarring tone of reprimand, considering that few had ever heard of the unitary executive.

What the unitary executive precept added to the separation of powers inquiry, Judge Silberman never made clear. "The Framers provided for a unitary executive to ensure that the branch wielding the power to enforce the law would be accountable to the people," he wrote. The convention rejected a "plural executive." In other words, the Founding Fathers' concept of "unity" had not changed: it still was all about having a single person, not a committee or a council, at the head of the executive branch. He and Madison and Hamilton agreed, but only on the narrow matter of a single-person executive officer.

When the case reached the Supreme Court, this allegedly bedrock phrase, in this important case, was not mentioned. Solicitor General Fried was asked only one question, on another subject, in his brief appearance supporting Olson, and he volunteered nothing on the unitary executive.

Nor was the talismanic phrase quoted by Chief Justice William Rehnquist when he delivered the Court's 7 to 1 judgment in *Morrison* v. *Olson*, reversing the D.C. Circuit and upholding the law.[24] The justices held that vesting the independent counsel's appointment in a court of law totally complied with the Constitution. Indeed, the federal courts for a century had made interim appointments during vacancies in the office of United States attorneys—an observation with relevance to the firing of at least eight prosecutors in George W. Bush's second term. Morrison was indeed an "inferior officer" for the purposes of the Constitution and did not need to be appointed by the president and confirmed by the Senate. Congress was not enhancing its own power at the executive's expense, nor was it diminishing executive authority in any significant way. The law hardly dented the president's Article II authority when it safeguarded her job by requiring that he not remove her without good cause. Rehnquist, in his relaxed way, announced that this just was not that big a deal.

Rehnquist's vote and his leadership in stiff-arming the unitarians has puzzled legal observers of all stripes but mostly confounded some of his conservative fans. He had been regarded as a supporter of executive power, especially in his time as assistant attorney general and as head of the Office of Legal Counsel, where so much of the legal theories of executive power were generated. Jay Bybee, who signed the "torture memo" and similar documents when he occupied that office, seemed mystified from his seat on the Ninth Circuit bench.[25] Tracing Rehnquist's Justice Department opinions, Bybee noted his rejection of President Nixon's assertion of inherent authority to impound congressionally enacted expenditures. "It may be argued that the spending of money is inherently an executive function, but the execution of any law is, by definition, an executive function, and it seems an anomalous proposition that because the Executive branch is bound to execute the laws, it is free to decline to execute them," said the Nixon loyalist and future chief justice.[26]

Although the chief justice apparently considered the unitary executive theory not worth debating, it was a very big deal for Justice Antonin Scalia. He was apoplectic in solitary dissent. He delivered large portions of a long opinion from the bench, starting with that epic quote from the Massachusetts constitution mentioned in the second chapter, the one purporting to hold the state—not the national government—to the strictest separation of powers.

For Justice Scalia to take as his text that eloquent passage from the Massachusetts constitution was incongruous. As Chief Justice Marshall famously said, "It is a Constitution we are expounding," but the Constitution was not that of a state but of the nation. Scalia continued, "The Framers of the Federal Constitution similarly viewed the principles of separation of powers as the absolutely central guarantee of a just Government." But that was not quite so, either. For one thing, Madison submitted a similar passage to the first Congress as a proposed part of the Bill of Rights, but the Congress declined to adopt it.[27]

Undeterred, Scalia quoted Madison's *Federalist* No. 47 for its florid tributes to separate powers, such as, "No political truth is certainly of greater intrinsic value, or is stamped with the authority of more enlightened patrons of liberty." Scalia stopped there, as many unitarians have. But Madison went on, showing how Massachusetts and every other state of the Confederation did indeed |divide its powers three ways—but blended them also|

Scalia soldiered along and his dissent became famous in part because he predicted, with political acuity, what might go wrong under the act. The appointment power might fall into the hands of judges "hostile to the administration," or a counsel who was a political foe of the president:

> The purpose of the separation and equilibration of powers in general, and of the unitary Executive in particular, was not merely to assure effective government but to preserve individual freedom. Those who hold or have held offices covered by the Ethics in Government Act are entitled to that protection as much as the rest of us. . . . It is, in other words, an additional advantage of the unitary Executive that it can achieve a more uniform application of the law.[28]

Those two references to the unitary executive, to which the chief justice gave no response, had a fatal judicial flaw. Scalia predicted what might go wrong yet admitted that the existing legal system did not always produce the uniformity desired by all. "Perhaps it is not always achieved, but the mechanism is there," he argued. Without admitting it, Scalia was weighing—from his judicial perch—the public values of two legal systems and clinging to his own policy preference for the conventional over Congress's special choice.

Two months after the Supreme Court decision, the prosecutor announced that she would not indict Olson.[29] In her report to the court that appointed her, she concluded that his disputed congressional testimony, "while not always forthcoming, was in our view literally true—and hence not subject to prosecution."[30]

The unitary executive initiative was not quite dead in the courts. There may have been a pulse, but Fried wrote that with *Morrison* "the whole enterprise ran aground and smashed to pieces."[31]

There remained what Charles Fried termed "the last episode in our separation-of-powers project," litigation over the strangely built United States Sentencing Commission. The Sentencing Reform Act of 1984 created the commission to cope with notorious disparities in punishment in the federal courts. Support was bipartisan, some supporters looking for an antidote to wide variations of sentencing and others looking for stiffer penalties.

The law created a five-member body to study and stratify the infinite ranges of penal code provisions and lay their proposed guidelines for judges before Congress, which had the ultimate power to approve, modify, or disapprove. The president appoints all seven commissioners, three of them federal judges picked from a list of six provided by the Judicial Conference of the United States, the judiciary's administrative and lobbying arm headed by the chief justice. To mollify judges who did not want to be seen as executive or congressional underlings, the law located the commission "in the judicial branch of the United States."

This odd structure was catnip for the Justice Department's remaining true believers in strictly separated powers, especially, according to Fried, Assistant Attorneys General John Bolton and Douglas Kmiec. Here was an agency of judges and laymen appointed by a president who had no power to supervise. An inconvenient factor, one that has not always deterred presidents from opposing laws they helped enact, was that the Reagan Justice Department had negotiated the system wholeheartedly with Senator Edward Kennedy and others in Congress. An even greater inconvenience is that the White House was among the many parts of government anxious to see this experiment successfully launched.

According to Fried's account, the true believers may have thought the law was unconstitutional, but the guidelines were to be defended as an exercise in presidential power "or they would not be defended at all."[32] In the waning days of the second Reagan term, with Meese gone and replaced by Dick Thornburgh, a former U.S. attorney and two-term governor of Pennsylvania, Fried held the strategic control, and with Thornburgh's approval set about defending the law. Bolton, head of the Civil Division and later ambassador to the United Nations, and Kmiec, head of the Office of Legal Counsel and later professor at Pepperdine Law School, "were determined to make one last stand for the 'muscular' and 'unitary' presidency. I was not. I could read. I had read the Independent Counsel case. I wanted to save the guidelines."[33] The whole exercise was especially odd considering that while the high strategists debated the powers of the Sentencing Commission, others within and without the Justice Department recognized that the important power transfer was to federal prosecutors, who received vastly enhanced discretion and, by their choices in bringing criminal charges, authority to compel guilty pleas from defendants.

Two days before Reagan left office, the Court ruled, 8 to 1, that the law and the guidelines were constitutional.[34] The truest believers along with Fried in fact most admired the dissent. Justice Scalia, who said now that the *Morrison* decision from last term looked "logical" by comparison, decried the creation of "a sort of junior-varsity Congress." He argued that there was "no place within our constitutional system for an agency created by Congress to exercise no governmental power other than the making of laws."

This was far from accurate, since Congress retained the last legislative word. In practice ever since, Congress has never hestitated to revise and reject proposed guidelines, usually in the direction of stiffer sentences.

No matter, to Fried the case "was bound to become another nail in the coffin of a rigorous view of the separation of powers. Whether the coffin is nailed up tight I cannot say, but I am not optimistic."[35]

5

THE PRESIDENTIALISTS, DOMESTIC AND GLOBAL

Radical as it is, the unitary executive theory that grew out of the Federalist Society and the Reagan Justice Department in the mid-1980s is tame and tepid when measured alongside the version that has gripped the administration of George W. Bush. This is the version most widely associated with Vice President Dick Cheney, his counsel and chief of staff David Addington, and John Yoo, principal draftsman of the most aggressive memoranda on the global reach of executive power.

How do the two versions compare? One answer comes from Steven G. Calabresi, the scholar most widely identified as the expounder of the unitary executive theory. He has written uncounted articles, filling thousands of pages, arguing for the theory and saluting the presidents that he finds are the heartiest champions. One huge batch of his law review articles surveyed all the presidents, in half-century bites, to prove that most presidents exhibited what he considered a major point: they may have been beaten back, but they never acquiesced in congressional power-stripping. (That is to say, unremarkably, that nearly all presidents have wanted to exercise power, especially when challenged, though they had not discovered the term unitary executive.)

What then of George W. Bush and his claims of immense authority to wage a war on terror from Baghdad to Chicago with expansive, inherent powers abroad and deeply intrusive techniques at home against aliens and citizens alike?

At the end of four law review articles spanning 688 eye-watering pages and 2,623 footnotes,[1] Calabresi arrived at the Bush administration and in the final two pages, said this:

> Support for the unitariness of the executive branch does not necessarily require supporting the broad claims of inherent executive authority advanced by the Bush Administration. Even Justice Antonin Scalia, whose dissent in *Morrison* v. *Olson* remains one of the definitive statements in support of the unitary executive, took the view that citizens detained as enemy combatants must be either charged with treason or be released, absent a congressional act suspending the right to habeas corpus. We agree with Justice Scalia on this point and think the Administration's doctrine of detaining citizens as enemy combatants takes the Lincolnian view of presidential emergency powers too far. As in the Steel Seizure Case, the Court was right in *Hamdi* to say that citizens cannot be deprived of life, liberty, or property without due process of law, even if the president has designated them to be enemy combatants in a war. As this Article has hopefully made clear, we generally reject such broad claims of presidential power to deprive people of life, liberty, or property in the absence of statutory authority. . . . [2]

So the unitary executive theory has more than one set of roots and more than one set of consequential policies. Without much question the theory's initial identity sprang from the Justice Department under Edwin Meese III in the middle to late 1980s. This carried the relatively modest banner, in hindsight at least, of repealing chunks of the New Deal, delegitimating administrative agencies, and taking back for the executive branch the supposedly usurped powers that had scattered among the agencies created by Congress.

The other main branch, which has come to be associated with Vice President Dick Cheney and his staff, and John Yoo and others at the Justice Department, traces to Cheney's experience as a young official in the Nixon administration and the Ford White House as he endured the humbling of the executive from Watergate and Congress's assertions of reform authority. And he puts greatest emphasis on his service as a dissenting congressman on the joint congressional committee that investigated the Iran-Contra affair.[3] Where a bipartisan majority found vast irregularities in the Iranian arms and hostages transactions and the use of cash proceeds to give forbidden aid to the contras in Nicaragua, Cheney found congressional meddling, statutory overreaching, and usurpation of the president's executive and foreign affairs prerogatives. He took pains to remind reporters of his nearly forgotten 1987 dissent.[4] He clearly still believed that "the Chief Executive will on occasion feel duty bound to assert monarchical notions of prerogative that will permit him to exceed the laws."

Others have traced Bush's claims to Richard Nixon's post-parting remarks to David Frost, regarding a discarded domestic surveillance plan that most would deem illegal: "Well, when the President does it that means it's not illegal." That remark, stunning then and stunning now, implied that not only could the president and his executors not be prosecuted, they also could not be impeached, which had already proved untrue as well as stunning. The Articles of Impeachment approved by the House Judiciary Committee on July 27, 1974, each accused Nixon of violating "his constitutional duty to take care that the laws be faithfully executed" (which of course underscores the argument that this portion of Article II is more of a duty than, as unitarians contend, a grant of power). Lest he give the impression that the president can "run amok," Nixon said the checks on the executive were that "a president has to come before the electorate"—not very useful in a second, lame-duck term of office—and the need to get appropriations from Congress, along with the limited disclosure of FBI and CIA actions to "trusted members of Congress."[5] (As it happens, Yoo, a leading provocateur of post–September 11 empowerment, argues that the remedy for those dissatisfied with executive war policies is cutting off funds. By contrast, Cheney has complained bitterly about the fund cutoffs that brought the Vietnam war to a close.) Cheney has not openly expressed approval of the Nixon statement, but he took many steps to create immunities for those who carried out presidential orders and policies.

Calabresi saw a silver lining in the Bush position in the power claims he criticized: "The fact the Bush Administration has made such extraordinary claims of presidential power—claims that go way beyond a claim of control over the removal and law execution powers defended in this Article—shows that there has been no acquiescence in any diminution in presidential power during the Administration of George W. Bush."

Thus Calabresi could award Bush the status of a stout unitarian by dint of the very excess he described: "The fact that at times Bush may have pushed an overly vigorous view of presidential power that expanded far beyond the logical boundaries of the unitary executive implicitly confirms his determination to defend the prerogatives of the executive branch."

That was Calabresi's mission, to survey and grade every president and enlist each as an exhibit to his theory. It is not always clear what even two centuries of presidents who wanted certain powers, such as the right to fire a Senate-confirmed cabinet officer without the help of the Senate, says about the Constitution. Yet in light of the excesses of the Bush administration, it is noteworthy that the unitary executive movement is not monolithic.

The Calabresis and the Yoos seem to make very little of their difference of opinion. There is no publicized rift among Federalist Society members, no featured internal debates at their conventions. Each camp maintains its quarrel with the conventional legal culture, but they might define unitary executive more clearly if they quarreled with each other.

6

THE PRESIDENTIALISTS, GLOBAL

John Yoo, the prolific, driven expounder of the more expansive version of the unitary executive theory, saw the presidency in decidedly royal terms. He argued in a 1996 law review article that, contrary to the understanding of most Americans, the Constitution's writers admired, not scorned, the war prerogatives of the British king.[1]

This was a primal, shocking misreading of basic American history. Yoo proclaimed that his view of the war powers framework created by the framers "differs sharply from that envisioned by modern scholars."

Contrary to the text of the Constitution's assignment to Congress of the power to declare war, Yoo claimed that the framers looked to England for a structure "designed to encourage presidential initiative in war." Approvingly noting that many American wars were undeclared, he said Congress's role was conferred "not by the Declare War Clause, but by its power over funding and impeachment." Its job was to fund a war, or if dissatisfied with it, to de-fund it.

The anti-royalist revulsion of the founding fathers is far from mere conventional wisdom. It is as American as the Boston Tea Party, as ingrained as the Declaration of Independence with its indictment of King George, as proud a part of the national heritage as the risk and sacrifice of the Revolutionary War. The record of the Constitutional Convention overflows with repudiation of the British king's authority to take his nation from peace to war.

35

As Chapter 2 demonstrated, Alexander Hamilton, the big fan of the energetic executive, came down foursquare against royalty in *The Federalist,* which the Federalist Society names itself after. What he argued, for efficiency and energy's sake, was for a single chief executive as opposed to a plural body. James Madison, whose silhouette the Federalist Society employs as a logo emblazoned on the neckties of its loyal members, was just as clear: "Those who are to *conduct a war* cannot in the nature of things, be proper or safe judges, whether *a war ought* to be *commenced, continued,* or *concluded."*[2]

Like many a Federalist Society–type of "Federalist," including Edwin Meese and Robert Bork, Yoo called himself an originalist, one who served the founders' original intent. Both branches of unitary executive thinking must stand or fall as originalist; that is, if the founding fathers did not envision the theory, then it must have developed somewhere else—by way of historic usage, through evolution under a "living" Constitution, or the imagination of the theorist. The problem with Yoo was not that he was an originalist, just that he twisted originalist history.

By the time Yoo joined the Federalist Society at Yale Law School in 1989,[3] the group cofounded by Calabresi was a going institution. Whether Yoo was already the domestic kind of "Federalist" at heart, he doubtless was aware of the domestic separation of powers litigation of *Morrison v. Olson.* Upon graduation in 1992 he clerked for Court of Appeals Judge Laurence H. Silberman, whose 1988 majority opinion, mentioning the unitary executive for the first time in federal court annals, had struck down the Independent Counsel Act but was reversed by the Supreme Court the same year. Two years later he served a term as a law clerk to Justice Clarence Thomas, who a decade later became the second Supreme Court justice to invoke the unitary executive by name, this time voting to sustain the more expansive, global argument of the executive branch.

In 1994 and 1995 Yoo was general counsel to the Senate Judiciary Committee under Republican chairman Orrin Hatch, a fond friend to Justice Thomas. Yoo taught law at the University of California at Berkeley, actively worked for George W. Bush in the Florida recount struggle, and joined the Justice Department in 2001 as deputy assistant attorney general in the Office of Legal Counsel, home of able lawyers who write legal policy memoranda for the administration. All this time, Yoo said little or nothing about what is called the milder unitary executive, placing his personal professional focus on diplomatic and foreign policy issues. Like his milder cousins, Yoo relied on an Article II executive power totally in the president's grasp, but with this extra wrinkle: the commander-in-chief power and all that might inhere in it, with echoes of Truman's assertions of inherent power when he seized the steel mills.

Charlie Savage, the *Boston Globe* reporter whose articles on Bush's power assertions and policies won a Pulitzer Prize, has plausibly explained Yoo's focus as a product of his family upbringing. Yoo was born in South Korea in 1967 and immigrated to the United States with his parents when he was a few months old. As Yoo stated in an interview with the *Korea Times* and to Savage, his parents' experience taught him that the Korean War, though often criticized as President Truman's war, undeclared and devoid of consultation with Congress, was a just and beneficial one that had spared them life under Communism.[4]

He was poised, then, to enlist in aid of presidential power when the nation suffered the September 11 attacks. Like his president, he rode a wave of belligerent national response. He produced reams of supportive drafts of legal opinions, and much of it went right to the White House without stopping at the attorney general's desk. Like many a house counsel, he told his client, the president, that he had a legal right to do what he wanted. Buttressed by a congressional resolution authorizing the use of military force,[5] yet maintaining that this legislative support was superfluous, Yoo asserted that since terror knew no boundaries, neither did the war on terror, justifying attacks at home or abroad anywhere the president saw danger.

Yoo produced a blizzard of executive branch memoranda based on, and often citing, his own idiosyncratic view of presidential power. They fed a network of committed lawyers and were warmly received by Cheney, Addington, and the White House counsel's office. They circulated them secretly for a couple of years, sheltering the documents from scholarly scrutiny until some of them leaked out and one of them underwent revision. It was a perfect storm of the theory of an academician and the disposition of a high government official in brief authority that supported Cheney's agenda for power and President Bush's temperament and world view.

On September 25, 2001, two weeks after the terrorist attacks, Yoo produced a memorandum opinion for the White House deputy counsel, Tim Flanigan.[6] Nobody questioned a president's right to retaliate immediately against an attack like September 11, but that understanding presupposed that, when time permitted, the president would check in with Congress about the state of hostilities and perhaps a declaration of war. Yoo wrote that the president may retaliate not only against the suspected attacker but also against foreign states suspected of harboring the attacker or terrorist organization. He may also "deploy military force preemptively" against terrorist organizations or harboring states "whether or not they can be linked to the specific incidents of September 11."[7] The president had "inherent executive powers that are unenumerated in the Consitution,"[8] the framers' aim being "a unity in purpose and energy in action."[9] Those overtones of the unitary executive, commander-in-chief variety, reappeared in subsequent memos. And citing his own law review article as authority, Yoo said, "During the period leading up to the Constitution's ratification, the power to initiate hostilities and to control the escalation of conflict had been long understood to rest in the hands of the executive branch."[10] As Louis Fisher has observed, the executive under the Articles of Confederation was not in a branch of its own, much less a source of unitary authority.[11]

When it came to detainees, Yoo and a colleague, Patrick Philbin, wrote the Pentagon's general counsel, William Haynes, on December 28, 2001, not only that the protections of the Geneva Conventions did not apply to al Qaeda and Taliban detainees, but also that the prison at Guantanamo Bay, Cuba, was beyond the reach of habeas corpus jurisdiction. Nor could Congress decree otherwise, for any such attempt "would represent a possible infringement on presidential discretion to direct the military."[12]

Perhaps the most brazen assertion of uncheckable power occurred in the core torture memo principally drafted by Yoo, signed by Assistant Attorney General Jay B. Bybee, and sent to White House counsel Alberto Gonzales. The memo was entitled "Standards of Conduct for Interrogation under 18 U.S.C. §§2340–2340A" (1994 criminal statutes implementing the Geneva Convention against torture).[13] Unilaterally defining away torture, the memo stated that a captor could commit "cruel, inhuman, or degrading" acts without violating the statute. To violate the law, and thus the Convention, would require infliction of "physical pain amounting to torture," which must be "equivalent in intensity to the pain accompanying serious physical injury, such as organ failure, impairment of bodily function, or even death."

The unitary executive philosophy already had carried the Bush administration a long way. The secret memos, some of which later became public, served as the defense brief for Washington war-makers to authorize what most Americans would deem torture and provide freedom from ultimate liability. Permission passed to Guantanamo Bay and the Abu Ghraib hellhole in Iraq. The efficacy of cruel and inhuman prisoner treatment as an anti-terror weapon is a rich subject beyond the scope of the power question. But public revulsion at this line of reasoning, on top of the revelations of sadistic techniques used at the Abu Ghraib prison in Iraq, did force the administration to moderate at least its tone in 2004. The Justice Department repudiated the torture memo, but not before Yoo's supervisor, Bybee, had been elevated to a prestigious appellate judgeship, while Yoo left Washington to return to Berkeley.

Now it was Yoo's turn to be outraged as he saw some of his handiwork scrapped. He lamented the White House's disavowal of his torture memo, calling it a needless retreat from principle.[14] More irritation was in the offing from the Supreme Court, where cases challenged the detentions and trials of "enemy combatants" though not their conditions of confinement.

In 2004 and again in 2006 the Court explicitly rejected the Bush unilateral stance. In 2004, in *Hamdi* v. *Rumsfeld*, the Court held that Yaser Esa Hamdi, an American citizen picked up on a battlefield in Afghanistan, must be given a chance to contest his enemy combatant status in some sort of competent tribunal.[15] Hamdi complained that his Guantanamo captors were denying him communication with the outside world and denying him a lawyer.

Justice Thomas alone agreed wholeheartedly with the Bush administration "unitary executive" argument that the powers of commander-in-chief should counsel courts to stay out of terrorism matters. Justice O'Connor, writing the controlling opinion for four justices, said, "We necessarily reject the government's assertion that separation of powers principles mandate a heavily circumscribed role for the courts in such circumstances."

That kind of deference, Justice O'Connor said, "serves only to condense power into a single branch of government," which of course was Bush's purpose. Even allowing that Congress's Authorization for the Use of Military Force put the nation at war, she declared, "a state of war is not a blank check for the President." And in a separate opinion

Justice David Souter added, "It is instructive to recall Justice Jackson's observation that the president is not commander in chief of the country, only of the military." That quote from the seminal concurring opinion in the Steel Seizure Case was another reminder that Jackson's self-described "oversimplified" hierarchy of situations affecting presidential power brooded over all the cases.

In another case, *Rasul* v. *Bush*,[16] the Court ruled 6 to 3 that prisoners at Guantanamo could file habeas corpus claims to challenge their detention status. The government had chosen the naval base in Cuba as its major detention site precisely because it was beyond United States borders, but the Court, quite realistically, said the base geographically was in Cuba—but under a tight, 101-year, perpetually renewable lease that gave the United States total control there.

Administration lawyers affected stunned surprise at this burst of judicial realism. They got Congress to amend the laws to define Guantanamo as specifically out of bounds. But two years later, in June 2006, the Court held in *Hamdan* v. *Rumsfeld*[17] that Congress had failed to cut off the habeas corpus rights of detainees at Guantanamo whose petitions were already on file. It went on to hold that the president's military commission system was at odds with what Congress had ordained in the form of the Uniform Code of Military Justice, another blow to unilateralism in the teeth of Congress's action. Finally, the Court held that the Geneva Conventions' so-called Common Article 3, requiring standards of humane treatment for war prisoners, applied to the captives such as those at Guantanamo.

Back at Berkeley, Yoo again was distressed. Now the high court justices were meddling with both the executive branch and Congress. "In an effort to interfere with the way the elected branches of our government have chosen to wage war against al-Qaeda," he wrote, "they interpreted a law recognizing military commissions to require the United States to follow what is known as 'Common Article 3' of the Geneva Conventions." "What the court is doing is attempting to suppress creative thinking," said Yoo. "The court has just declared that it's going to be very intrusive in the war on terror. They're saying, 'We're going to treat this more like the way we supervise the criminal justice system.'"[18]

The Court, citing lack of adequate congressional authority for what the president had set up, virtually invited Congress to supply the missing law if it wanted to, yet Yoo saw nothing but judicial interference. His lament had this much justification from his point of view: the Court's insistence that the administration must seek relief from Congress was an utter repudiation of the unitary executive theory of unilateral authority.

In Washington, the administration did go back to Congress seeking relief. Theodore B. Olson, who had been solicitor general from 2001 to June 2004, through the first round of enemy combatant cases, sharply criticized the *Hamdan* decision, but within weeks was testifying before the Senate Judiciary Committee urging legislative fixes, noting the Court's own invitation. He said Congress should restore the status quo that preceded the *Rasul* decision, putting Guantanamo off limits for prisoner habeas corpus petitions, and should expressly authorize a military commission system.

Days after Bush signed the Military Commission Act of 2006, Yoo's mood swung back to triumphal.[19] Press and pundits had missed the big story. It was not that the presidency had won. "Instead, it is the judiciary that lost. . . . The new law is, above all, a stinging rebuke to the Supreme Court. It strips the courts of jurisdiction to hear any habeas corpus claim filed by any alien enemy combatant anywhere in the world. It was passed in response to the effort by a five-justice majority in *Hamdan* v. *Rumsfeld* to take control over terrorism policy." The *Hamdan* decision "was an unprecedented attempt by the court to rewrite the law of war and intrude into war policy. The court must have thought its stunning power grab would go unchallenged."

Since the *Hamdan* opinions expressly contemplated that Congress might well agree to administration requests, and while many in Congress voted in anger or disagreement with the Supreme Court's interpretation of the law, Yoo's op-ed article was, for such a serious subject, hilarious. Perhaps still angry at the White House for acquiescing in the Justice Department's repudiation of his torture memos, and perhaps unaccustomed to the notion of executive-legislative power sharing, Yoo overlooked Justice Stephen Breyer's plain statement for four concurring justices: "The Court's conclusion ultimately rests upon a single ground: Congress has not issued the Executive a 'blank check.' Indeed, Congress has denied the President the legislative authority to create military commissions of the kind at issue here. Nothing prevents the President from returning to Congress to seek the authority he believes necessary."[20]

For several months it appeared that the president's own party would create high hurdles for legislation. John Warner, chairman of the

Senate Armed Services Committee, joined with Senators John McCain and Lindsey Graham to assert the need to protect some prisoner rights and prevent abuses. McCain, who famously was a prisoner of war for five years during the Vietnam War, stressed the need for high standards lest the United States invite more brutality against captured Americans. Graham, a sometime specialist in military law, stressed the model of the Uniform Code of Military Justice, since the *Hamdan* decision might have been unnecessary if Bush had utilized courts-martial.

Democrats, reluctant in the election season to appear pro-terrorist, used the Republicans for political shelter, joining to report a moderate bill from the Armed Services Committee in early September. The bill passed the Senate overwhelmingly, but hawks in the House and the White House combined to produce a House-Senate conference measure that was substituted for the Senate's work, and the Senate acquiesced. Judiciary chairman Arlen Specter, who had verbally championed habeas corpus rights, narrowly lost a vote to guarantee them for the alien combatants, yet he voted for the flawed final bill. Some Democrats realized that their reliance on the Republicans had been misplaced, and suddenly the final legislative product was riddled with repressive measures.

The Military Commission Act of 2006 had every sign of being the blank check the Court had found missing. It authorized and legitimized the commissions that Bush's lawyers were designing. It gave Bush permission to identify the defendants, imprison them, and interrogate them, albeit with a few limitations at the extreme. The law declared that a commission "is a regularly constituted court, affording all the necessary 'judicial guarantees which are recognized as indispensable by civilized peoples' for purposes of common Article 3 of the Geneva Conventions." If that was not valid enough, it authorized the president to interpret the conventions and required only that he publish his interpretations. If that was not secure enough, the law simply states that no designated unlawful enemy combatant may invoke Geneva anyway. And besides, anyone designated an alien unlawful combatant now had no right to go to court with a habeas corpus petition or any other complaint. He simply must await his designation, which is subject to a narrow review, and then his trial, if any, or release, or somehow an end to the war on terror.

7

THE WILL AND PLEASURE
OF THE PRESIDENT

The unitary executive way of thinking can lead to other kinds of excesses beyond the royalistic war-making claims of power. Habits of secrecy and of hoarding information; the jealous assertion of the exclusive right to decide; and the refusal to share or cooperate with other branches—all these breed the failures of insularity, including arrogance, that beget inefficiency and rewards incompetence.

Such is the experience of the Bush administration. Its enhanced anti-terrorist eavesdropping program (which was dubbed the Terrorism Surveillance Program, or simply "The Program") flouted an already permissive Foreign Intelligence Surveillance Act (FISA), when more candid dealings with Congress probably would have accomplished the goals. Even when the president had the undoubted power to replace any and all of the ninety-four United States attorneys who serve at his pleasure, even then the White House and Justice Department disgraced themselves by their choice of methods and utter incompetence in the execution. Oddly, considering the Bush administration's valid claim to high authority to fire top prosecutors without cause, neither George W. Bush nor Attorney General Gonzales admitted to handling the problem personally, pretending that the firings pretty much ran themselves through underlings. Crudely, the administration has replaced presumptions of openness with presumptions of secrecy over information that is public and should be free. It has suppressed important information that Congress needed and deserved. Building on a phony and fraudulent doctrine of state secrets, Bush and Cheney have told judges that they must not even peek at alleged national security information that might decide a citizen's case. And it took an abusive use of the unquestioned presidential pardoning power to spare Cheney's lieutenant the consequences of his hubristic lies to investigators in the intelligence leak case concerning Valerie Plame.

"Decision, activity, secrecy and dispatch," those Hamiltonian virtues of an energetic executive, demand much more than ironclad commandeering, ill-prepared execution, and information vacuums. Energy wasted on trying to maintain secrecy would be better spent applying tact and negotiation.

The climate of conventional search and surveillance has always been highly favorable to government, and the realm of FISA is even more so. The Fourth Amendment prohibits only "unreasonable" searches, so ordinary searches in criminal cases are easily approved by the courts, either on warrants or by carved-out exceptions to warrant requirements. In the four decades since Congress authorized wiretap warrants for federal law enforcement, the annual reports show the judges rarely if ever deny approval. The secret FISA court seems no less compliant, partly because, as with conventional warrants, the hard job of drafting credible applications is done by Justice Department specialists. If speed is needed, the FISA court will entertain after-the-fact warrant applications. If the going still gets tough, Congress will relax the law's strictures, as it has many times since FISA was enacted in 1978.

Why then did the Bush administration, rather than ask Congress for permission, unilaterally embark upon The Program of surveillance between foreign and domestic communicants in 2002? Most likely because it could—or assumed it could. The unilateralist executive does not enjoy asking leave. Stories have indicated that some officials had word, or merely feared, that Congress would arbitrarily refuse permission. Even so, executive officials claim to have briefed Senate and House intelligence committee members, but some members have claimed that the briefings were conducted in a rapid "drive-by" manner that masked the legal and constitutional issues of The Program.

The hubris of White House unitarians produced the crude, scandalous 2004 visit to the hospital bed of the ailing Attorney General John Ashcroft. Ashcroft had temporarily yielded his attorney general authority to his deputy, James Comey, who in turn had refused to endorse renewal of The Program, or some aspect of it. Andrew Card, the White House chief of staff, and Alberto Gonzales, the counsel and future attorney general, did not let concern for the seriously sick Ashcroft interfere with their unfeeling and unsuccessful attempt to overrule Comey, who arrived to witness the calamitous scene. Comey testified to Congress that, later that evening, Card said of the visit, "We were just there to wish him well."[1]

The Card-Gonzales intrusion was not illegal or unconstitutional, yet for Gonzales it was part of his baggage of deficits, including fibbing and fencing with inquiring congressional committees, that led to his resignation as attorney general just before Labor Day 2007.

Similarly, the sacking of half a dozen high-ranking Justice Department officials—almost as numerous as the cashiered United States attorneys during Bush's second term—sprang from an action apparently within the conceded constitutional power of the president. The regional prosecutors serve "at the pleasure of the President," which means the chief executive can dismiss any of them for no reason. That is what the administration and its defenders said over and over as the suggested reasons oozed out amid confused, incredible, and gratuitous claims of underperformance. The moral is, do not do everything you have a right to do, which is part of the larger moral for the global unitarians, do not do everything you think you have the power to do. For Gonzales, the moral is, do not get caught falsely denying that you took part in this mess, and do not go down as the attorney general who could not remember much.

The Gonzales Justice Department hatched the U.S. attorney replacement program with the knowledge that Congress had unwittingly made it easier to bypass Senate confirmation for many of the new appointees. A Justice Department official drafted, and a Specter aide quietly inserted in the 2005 Patriot Act reauthorization bill, a provision giving interim appointees to U.S. attorney positions a virtually unlimited time in office without Senate confirmation. That provision replaced a century-old law by which local district judges could fill vacancies when they lasted as long as 120 days. Asked by Senator Dianne Feinstein who thought up the change, Attorney General Alberto Gonzales testified that he had no recollection of the law change, but he did testify that he supported the idea "not in order to avoid Senate involvement, but because I, quite frankly, do not like the idea of the Judiciary deciding who serves on my staff. And that's why I supported the law."[2]

Others, perhaps truer believers in the unitary executive, had more reason to erase the old law. In *Morrison* v. *Olson*, Chief Justice Rehnquist had used the old law to answer the argument that it was incongruous, and thus unconstitutional, for a judge to appoint an independent counsel. He noted that judges made these interim appointments all the time.[3] Recall that the *Morrison* decision ranks near the defeat of Supreme Court nominee Robert Bork among the beasts of Federalist Society lore. There remain unanswered questions, including why senators such as Feinstein and Specter nodded when they should have been guarding their patronage, but Congress restored the old law and Bush signed the repeal in June 2007.[4]

The restoration of the old interim appointment structure was accomplished with no resistance from the administration and little investigation in either the Senate or House, probably to avoid calling attention to Congress's inattentiveness to the stealthy change that deprived senators of their valued role in helping the White House choose the top federal prosecutors in their states.

Policies and practices of the Bush administration were also within the formal powers under the Freedom of Information Act, the guiding statute. But the regulation telling federal departments to treat information requests under the presumption of maintaining secrecy[5] was of a piece with the administration's approach to government in the other contested realms, such as war-waging regulations. The same applies to the administration's rule that carves a huge hole in the 1988 Public Records Preservation Act. That act requires the release of documents after a dozen years in secrecy, but the White House decreed that former presidents and their families could block release simply by objecting.[6]

Similarly, it probably was within the formal power of the White House to forbid a health economist to tell members of Congress the true cost of the drug prescription Medicare benefit they were voting on.[7] There are valid reasons, ordinarily, for management to try to control the message it sends to Congress. But it is a civic sin when Congress is denied the information it needs, and the public pays for, to legislate. It is an abuse of power at best, a sorry exercise of the unitary executive's internal control function.

The State Secrets Privilege, a rule that sounds venerable but actually is only about a half-century old, allows federal officials to plead successfully that a trial judge should not even look at some evidence in a claim of danger to national security. The doctrine stems from a 1953 Supreme Court decision, *United States* v. *Reynolds*.[8] In that case the widows of civilian engineers killed in a plane crash were thrown out of court when the government moved to suppress an accident report on grounds that it contained military secrets. The Supreme Court held the claim sufficient to prevent the trial judge from examining the material secretly in chambers. If he had done so, he would have seen what emerged many years later: that the government's claim was fraudulent. This power to seal up evidence of negligence or wrongdoing has suited many administrations over the years while the Court sits by timidly. The Bush administration has expanded the no-peek power to a new low threshold, well below national security, when the courts agreed with lawyers for Dick Cheney not even to allow a trial judge to look at secret information about the Vice President's energy task force.[9] Unfortunately the state secrets privilege, replete with its distrust of judges that denies litigants the right to have a judge look at the privileged evidence in secret, survived a recent challenge in the Supreme Court,[10] and it remains unexamined.

Finally, in this sampling of unitarian excesses there is a strange twist to the old argument against the appointment of special counsel with freedom to investigate, and prosecute or exonerate, high officials when the attorney general has a disqualifying conflict of interest. Chapter 4 described how the law that created court-appointed independent counsels from outside of government was upheld by the Supreme Court. The challengers claimed that the appointment would be an intrusion on the unitary executive unless the counsel was appointed and removable without cause by the president. The rationale for the law was that the president and his high aides should not be allowed to exonerate themselves if the rule of law was to be respected.

In the celebrated Valerie Plame leak case, it appeared that divulging the name of an undercover CIA agent was an outrage and might be a crime. Exit Attorney General John Ashcroft, who recognized that it would be unthinkable for him to head an investigation that would accuse, or exonerate, the likes of a Dick Cheney or someone near cabinet rank. Ashcroft recused himself, and his deputy, Jim Comey, recused himself also, after appointing the U.S. attorney in Chicago, the widely respected Patrick Fitzgerald, giving him the added duty of special counsel free of any supervision by politically appointed officials. Lawyers cried foul, as did supporters of I. Lewis (Scooter) Libby, chief of staff to Cheney who was convicted of perjury and obstruction of justice for lying to investigators and a grand jury about his own leaking. The foul? Fitzgerald should have been appointed and removable by the president, a status he already held in his regular job in Chicago. To challenge the appointment of a Justice Department subordinate on separation of powers grounds was to turn the unitary executive arguments, already standing on their heads, on their sides.

The final touch was the presidential pardon of Libby while his conviction was on appeal. Bush found the prison time meted out to Libby, thirty months, excessive, so he commuted all prison time, while leaving his $250,000 fine intact. Bush, of course, with his undisputed power to pardon or commute, could have reduced the jail term to any shorter one. By wiping out all jail time, he necessarily decided that for the crime of lying to the FBI and a grand jury, obstructing an investigation into whether anyone committed a crime, *any* imprisonment, even a few months, would be excessive for the vice president's chief of staff.

8

SIGNING STATEMENTS

O nce upon a time, presidential signing statements, if uttered at all, were ribbon-cutting love-ins proclaiming success, and opportunities to give pens to the legislators who had done so much to make this day possible. Not so much any more. Now, even when there has been a Rose Garden or Oval Office hand-shaker, it is prudent to watch for a signing statement, a declaration that might say how much of the new law the president will honor or enforce.

George W. Bush has done this more than all previous forty-two presidents combined. He has indicated that he will not enforce all or parts of more than seven hundred provisions of law. Signing statements—even some signing statements of that kind—are not all bad, but Bush has given them a bad name.

Probably the worst acts of White House abuse of signing statements were Bush's dealings with Senator John McCain and his anti-torture bill in late 2005. Against a backdrop of the Abu Ghraib scandal, the exposure and partial repudiation of administration memoranda justifying what everyone but the administration called torture, McCain added an amendment to a Defense Department money bill forbidding the torture of detainees anywhere in the world. He gathered massive support in both houses, sufficient to overwhelm Bush's veto threat, whereupon Bush called a momentary, deceptive truce. He summoned McCain for an announced agreement to the torture ban. Bush signed the bill, by now expanded to a politically plum package of hurricane and flu relief. Then he issued a Friday evening statement, timed to lull press and public to boredom or deeper slumber—this one two days before the New Year—stating that he reserved the right to ignore this law.

In the parlance of the art of signing statements, all the words after "shall construe" are the killers. As in, "The executive branch shall construe" provisions for detainees "in a manner consistent with the constitutional authority of the President to supervise the unitary executive branch and as Commander in Chief and consistent with the constitutional limitations on the judicial power."[1]

This bill being a must-pass, veto-proof, many-faceted money measure, the signing statement used "shall construe" a dozen times in all. Some of the objections concerned the classic struggle, common to presidents and congresses, over alleged attempts by committee chairs to resurrect the meddlesome legislative veto in new disguises. Others resisted legislative directives over expenditures that Bush, like other presidents, said he would treat with respect but as "advisory" in nature rather than commanding.

Should McCain have been surprised by this political and personal betrayal? Probably not. Democrats were furious, if only for the loss of a safeguard for which McCain, the survivor of captivity in Vietnam, was providing political cover. They littered the Supreme Court confirmation hearings of Samuel A. Alito, Jr.,[2] with questions about his 1986 role in the move to promote signing statements as part of legislative history. They also quizzed him about his endorsement of the unitary executive concept as late as 2000 in a speech to the Federalist Society.

Alito managed in his testimony to avoid discussion about the strength of signing statements in the scheme of court interpretation of laws, but a pride of law professors has argued all sides of the matter. As for his belief in the unitary executive theory, he cast himself as of the domestic, Calabresi school of thought as opposed to the grander, global, John Yoo school of unilateral, inherent executive war power. "The Question of the unitary executive," he testified, "does not concern the scope of executive powers, it concerns who controls whatever power the executive has."[3]

Charles Fried, veteran of the unitary wars, testified for Alito's authenticity against his Harvard colleague, Laurence H. Tribe, who argued that Alito's public statements were open to the global interpretation. In his prepared testimony, Tribe denounced the unitary executive theory as "a gerry-rigged contraption cooked up with straightedge and scissors by people who had read the Constitution's text and certain canonical Federalist Papers but little else on the subjejct." The donnish witnesses were having a merry debate when the Judiciary Committee broke for a floor vote. When the senators returned, it was time for another panel of witnesses, alas.[4]

Alito went on to Senate confirmation, but the legislators were only beginning to wrestle with signing statements, spurred by a series of articles by Charlie Savage of the *Boston Globe.*

The heart of the series, which ran occasionally from January through November 2006, was an April 30 story, "Bush Challenges Hundreds of Laws; President Cites Powers of His Office." The series ultimately counted signing statements for 125 bills to date, containing challenges to a more than 750 individual provisions. Other sources, academic and journalistic, had varying tallies, but it was clear enough that the practice, begun with one signing statement in the James Monroe administration, had grown over the generations, accelerating with Ronald Reagan and with a leap under George W. Bush. An American Bar Association task force, later supported by the association's House of Delegates, condemned the statements, arguing that presidents should sign bills or veto them and not issue what amounts to an unconstitutional line-item veto of selective disapproval.[5] That view was sharply disputed by Walter Dellinger, head of the Office of Legal Counsel under Bill Clinton, and other alumni of the office, from both parties. Like the others, Dellinger was accustomed to making legal arguments for their presidents. He specifically rejected the idea that a president, handed a bill of hundreds of pages, must always sign or veto only. The problem was not with the practice of signing statements, he said, but rather the extreme content of some of them.[6]

Arlen Specter, the future former chairman of the Senate Judiciary Committee, called a hearing on June 27, 2006. Specter, a casualty of White House dealings over torture and surveillance by intelligence agencies—and soon to be a casualty of administration obduracy about habeas corpus for prisoners in the war on terror—was as impatient as any Democrat with the Justice Department witness, Deputy Attorney General Michelle E. Boardman, who defended her president. She said Bush's practice was not radically different from that of recent presidents, increasingly caught in national security areas of contention. She denied any intention to evade laws: "A constitutional signing statement . . . is not a declaration that the President will not follow the appointments provisions, but that he remains free to abide by them as a matter of policy."

Presidents, no less than legislators or courts, have a duty to interpret the Constitution as part of their duty to obey it, Boardman said. Some of the bills tangled directly with the executive's attempts to manage classified information. Many others, a surprising number, violated the ban on legislative vetoes declared by the Supreme Court in 1983. And yes, the scholarly works of Calabresi showed that virtually all presidents strived to maintain their rightful powers and that at least since Franklin D. Roosevelt they saw themselves as fully empowered heads of the executive branch. Besides, she testified, the practice "is an ordinary part of a respectful constitutional dialogue between the branches."[7]

Senator Specter was especially ready for that argument about dialogue, raising very good questions: What about the negotiations that preceded the McCain torture bill and the Bush signing statement? What about the government's agreement with Congress to report on the use of their expanded surveillance, disparaged by Bush in his signing statement on the Patriot Act Reauthorization bill?

Oddly, although Bush reserved the right to disregard the law's obligation to keep track and report back on the use of surveillance measures such as expanded so-called National Security Letters to compel information from citizens, the administration *did* comply with the law, in its fashion. The Justice Department's inspector general, Glen A. Fine, reported in March 2007 that his investigators had indeed complied with the law's demand to investigate the search practices—only to find the compliance shoddy and spotty, and more invasive than necessary of individual privacy rights, to the chagrin even of Republicans on the House Judiciary Committee. FBI director Robert S. Mueller III confirmed the deficiencies and promised to fix them.[8]

Why did the Justice Department comply, after all, with the law's reporting requirements? Partly because conservative legislators then in control of Congress had demanded an accounting, and likely also because of the disposition to comply and to enforce compliance exhibited by Inspector General Fine. And why was the FBI so remiss in implementing the search power, as Fine made clear in his report? Probably because of traditional, institutional FBI resistance to outside authority, encouraged by a presidential signing statement signaling that faithful compliance was discretionary.

Two days after the Senate hearing, by coincidence, Justice Antonin Scalia, famous for his sometimes fair charge that lawyers and judges abuse legislative history, oddly chided his brethren in a Guantanamo case for paying no attention to a Bush signing statement. In his dissent in *Hamdan* v. *Rumsfeld,* he wrote, "Of course in its discussion of legislative history the Court wholly ignores the President's signing statement, which explicitly set forth *his* understanding that the DTA [Detainee Treatment Act] ousted jurisdiction over pending cases."[9]

As the debate in Congress should indicate, no side has all the truth. There surely are "good" signing statements and "bad" ones. Gerald Ford was within his rights to sign the 1974 Campaign Reform Act, which was so complex and intricate that it posed two dozen novel constitutional questions for the Supreme Court. But he was also right to complain upon signing that the law's appointments to the Federal Election Commission were infirm because a sticky-fingered Congress gave itself two appointments. Congress distrusted the executive branch to administer the campaign law, but it is an executive job under the Constitution and the Supreme Court so held.[10]

Similarly, President Reagan was justified in complaining, as he signed the Gramm-Rudman-Hollings budget balancing law, that the comptroller general, the linchpin in the law's scheme, owed his job to Congress and was out of place, constitutionally speaking. As discussed in Chapter 4, the Justice Department and some private attorneys so persuaded the high court.

On the other hand, George H. W. Bush issued one signing statement that could make his son look like a statesman. After a series of Supreme Court decisions denying employment benefits to minorities and women under Title VII of the Civil Rights Act, moderate Republicans led the way to passage of the Civil Rights Restoration Act of 1991. The elder Bush, seeking to appease his party's right wing, opposed the bill as a "quota bill" and vetoed one version. The rights coalition stormed back with a veto-proof majority. The key provision made it harder for businesses, once the plaintiffs showed a disproportionally low minority work force, to assert a defense of business necessity. After a gala Rose Garden signing ceremony, Bush released a statement citing a legal memorandum by opponents of the bill and said their view of business necessity was authoritative.[11]

Happily for civil rights forces, Bush's attempts to redirect civil rights activities of his bureaucracy were unsuccessful and short-lived, as was his remaining time in office. He made few friends left or right and, in any case, the law as written survived. Senator John Danforth, a chief Republican sponsor of the bill, called the White House maneuver a serious mistake. It reminded him of a scene from the movie *Fatal Attraction*, in which the Glenn Close character, presumed dead, lunges from a bathtub with a knife in her hand.[12]

Early in 2007 John Conyers, Jr., the new chairman of the House Judiciary Committee, launched hearings and an investigation into the consequences of signing statements. The first results, in a Government Accountability Office report, showed a mixed pattern of compliance with statutes and possible yielding to noncompliance in obedience to signing statements. Plainly, the pursuit of patterns of adherence to law and executive resistance will be labor-intensive.[13]

Presidential signing statements are here to stay because they have significant uses and abuses. They provide a platform for White House messages, though often they are hidden in after-hours news releases or in the plain sight of small print in government publications. For a president forced, for one reason or another, to sign a bill he thinks harbors unconstitutional provisions, they can be an effective defensive weapon. They can be offensive weapons too—in-your-face backtalk to a hostile Congress. They can clarify or confuse, anger or bore. They can usefully help the president direct or misdirect subordinates who must carry out the law, although an executive order will do as well. Above all, despite the Justice Department's claim that they are "not about power,"[14] they are decidedly about power. As Samuel Alito wrote to his Justice Department strategy group in 1986, they are about "the power of the executive to shape the law."[15]

9

Theory and Consequence

The unitary executive has come a long way for a theory that has a hole in its heart and no basis in history or coherent thought. It simply is devoid of content, not expressed or even strongly implied in foundational documents such as *The Federalist*, not to mention the Constitution. If "energy in the executive" meant overpowering force, or if Hamilton's "unity" meant unitary executive rather than a one-person chief executive, the unitarians might have the makings of a case based on originalism and history, but all that appears upon inspection is a heartfelt yearning for the founding documents to mean more than they say. This applies to both branches of the theory as they have evolved, the domestic and bureaucratic brand of exclusive executive control, and the global, royal, commander-in-chief unilateralist variety.

Supreme Court decisions have twice demolished the unitary executive as a matter of constitutional reason, first in *Morrison* v. *Olson* in 1988 and then in *Hamdan* v. *Rumsfeld* in 2006. *Morrison* shattered the claim that the vesting of "the executive power" in a president under Article II of the Constitution created a hermetic unit free from checks and balances apart from the political community. It firmed up the power of Congress to shape executive departments and adjust presidential controls according to their mission, and safeguarded the independent administrative agencies from subordination to the White House. *Hamdan* reaffirmed that the unitary executive claims for unilateral, royalist power are not the

American way of governing. The rule, espoused by many justices over time but ingeniously and simply described by Justice Jackson in the Steel Seizure case, requires presidential interaction with Congress: "The actual art of governing under our Constitution does not and cannot conform to judicial definitions of the power of any of its branches based on isolated clauses or even single Articles torn from context. . . . Presidential powers are not fixed but fluctuate, depending upon their disjunction or conjunction with those of Congress."[1]

So the Supreme Court has reset the checks and balances, yet the national executive has remained unchecked and unbalanced.[2] This is mainly because the Bush administration has pressed an agenda in which power itself has always been one of the main objectives, while Congress, partly from political deadlock and largely for lack of institutional energy, has simply rolled over.

The pursuit of "presidential power for its own sake" was integral to every Bush administration action that came to the attention of Jack Goldsmith, the conservative scholar who headed the Justice Department's Office of Legal Counsel in 2003 and 2004.[3] Despite sympathy for the administration's war aims and even some of its methods, Goldsmith found himself unable to support the Yoo-generated torture memo of August 1, 2002, and an undisclosed number of others as well. He found Yoo's writings poorly reasoned, even "wildly broader than was necessary to what was actually being done."[4] Goldsmith ridiculed Yoo's definition of torture as inducing a near-death experience by noting that key terms were lifted from a totally unrelated statute covering eligibility for medical benefits.[5] When brought to public view, the Justice memos "made it seem as though the administration was giving official sanction to torture," and brought "dishonor to the United States."[6]

Goldsmith, who resigned after officially repudiating the memos, blamed several factors, among them genuine fear of terrorist attacks and an evolving legal culture that encouraged hindsighted recriminations and criminal liability for actions that might later be deemed unlawful. Additionally he blamed pressure from the White House, dominated in the detail work by David Addington, whose "judgments were crazy."[7] The net effect of the Bush unilateralism, Goldsmith concluded, was to weaken the presidency, quite the opposite effect intended by the Cheney-Addington programs.

Goldsmith's attempts to clean up the government's policy on harsh interrogation bordering on torture seemed destined to prove temporary only. On October 4, 2007, the *New York Times* reported that after Goldsmith's departure his successor, Steven Bradbury, secretly signed an Office of Legal Counsel memo restoring authority for the harsh techniques.[8]

To give credit to the Bush-Cheney lawyers and lobbyists, once the high court had made the rules plain in the *Hamdan* decision, they applied the *Youngstown* formula of interdependence and sought—and obtained—from Congress the powers the Court said were unavailable unilaterally. Congress did not kick the Court, as John Yoo triumphally declared. The administration sensibly read *Hamdan* as both a demand and an invitation to seek out Congress. Congress then gave Bush all he asked, including the authority to write his own rules for compliance with the Geneva Conventions, and creating the military commissions. An obedient Congress also virtually abolished habeas corpus, trying to exclude any useful judicial review, for detainees.

Such a transfer of power makes the constitutional landscape look much as it did when Bush and Cheney launched their civic aggressions, at least politically, since in theory Congress could always try to undo its obliging work. Through no virtue or energy of its own, Congress has won the power and a stake in the unitary executive fight. Will Congress achieve health and energy in its own right to establish balance and checks?

While waiting for Congress, anyone hoping that a regime change in the White House would cure matters might be dreaming. A new president of any party might well inventory the accumulated powers—and claims of power—and decide to try hanging on to them. Presidents do not easily surrender authority, even if they recognize that the authority was illegitimately claimed.

Yet presidential candidates must be asked their view of these questions, whether they understand them and whether they can identify any Bush administration claims they could envision renouncing. That issue has begun to emerge. In a debate among Republican candidates, contestants were asked whether the president could unilaterally bomb or invade Iran or whether he would need Congress's assent.[9] Hillary Clinton, accusing the Bush-Cheney administration of a "power grab," said in an interview with the *Guardian* newspaper that she would "absolutely" renounce some of Bush's claims of unilateral power, though she said the specifics must await "a review that I undertake when I get to the White House," an only partly reassuring stance, but a modest beginning.[10]

Any new president had better be realistic about the way those powers are flexed, even undisputed powers. For example, the White House travel office staff served "at the pleasure of the President," but arbitrary firings brought shame to the early Clinton administration. Similarly, United States attorneys serve "at the pleasure of the President," yet arbitrary, bungling, insulting dismissals can ignite investigations and firings of more higher officers, including the attorney general himself, than of those initially dismissed. Absolute power, including undisputed executive power, corrupts absolutely, in more ways than one.

Is Congress worth waiting for? One test of worthiness would be whether Congress, if only to restore its own honor, recaptures the habeas corpus rights it gave away in the Military Commission Act of 2006. By stripping access to federal courts for detainees, Congress may have compounded constitutional violations beyond all court remedies. Article I, Section 9, says, "The privilege of the writ of habeas corpus shall not be suspended, unless when in cases of rebellion or invasion the public safety may require it." The administration claims that all the world is the battlefield in the terror war, but there is no pending claim of rebellion or invasion. So while the illegitimacy of Congress's elimination of the writ is plain, the question is whether the Supreme Court will find a way to reach the issue.

The Supreme Court may yet revive the Great Writ and rescue the Constitution and Congress from Congress's craven behavior. Though litigation is sometimes difficult to mount, it has never been true, contrary to John Yoo's constitution, that "the courts have no role whatsoever."[12] With the encouragement of Federalist Society allies, a rightward-veering Court has not been shy about asserting itself—disturbingly in commerce clause cases,[13] alarmingly in decisions restricting legislative enforcement of Fourteenth Amendment values,[14] and notoriously in *Bush v. Gore*,[15] halting the recount of the 2000 presidential election and the operation of the regular constitutional machinery for electing the president. When a justice can cast the deciding vote to halt the recount with the explanation that irreparable damage would ensue for candidate Bush and the country "by casting a cloud upon what he claims to be the legitimacy of his election,"[16] we have a decidedly interventionist Supreme Court, one that should not blink at declaring what the law of habeas corpus is.

Congress must, as usual, reform itself.[17] In both houses and in both political parties, it needs numerous members willing to recognize White House assaults and stand up to them. Mere partisan battling will not save the institutions, but however it is accomplished, the Senate, for example, needs to guard the Supreme Court from nominees who excessively worship the executive branch, whether or not they subscribe to the unitary executive theory. As it is, Justices Scalia and Thomas have invoked the theory, Justice Alito has celebrated it in the past, and Chief Justice John G. Roberts voted with the Court of Appeals majority that the Supreme Court overturned in the *Hamdan* decision. The Senate, which nodded in letting the Justice Department appoint "interim" United States attorneys for virtually unlimited terms, needs to guard against such end runs, including many recess appointments. The Senate's Democratic majority made a good start by convening pro forma floor sessions during the 2007 Thanksgiving Break[18]

Both houses must continue to pursue inquiries like the United States attorney cases and other power abuses, and learn institutional vigilance, guarding against abuses, without regard to party affiliation. Legislators must demand information and proof of need before surrendering any more authority for surveillance of Americans. And if the White House insists on issuing voluminous, open-ended, and cryptic signing statements to legislation, both houses should call the occupants over to explain the ambiguities and state whether and how they are enforcing the laws they claim the right to "construe" out of existence.

The nomination of Michael Mukasey to succeed Alberto Gonzales as attorney general created a new theater for the contest over power. Originally greeted as a rescuer of the Justice Department from ignominy, incompetence, mendacity, and blind obedience to White House commands, Mukasey stirred unease among Democrats and moderate Republicans, chiefly over the specifics of one form of torture. Ultimately, the Senate's hope for a competently led, law-abiding Justice Department prevailed over its revulsion at Mukasey's refusal to declare that the interrogation technique of waterboarding amounted to unconstitutional, illegal torture.

Mukasey, a retired federal judge with wide legal experience and acquaintance with terrorism-related issues, was nominated September 17, 2007, and confirmed November 8 by a vote of 53 to 40. His confirmation hearings aroused an increasingly engaged body of senators.

Mukasey pleased many by declaring, for instance, that he found Jack Goldsmith's book, *The Terror Presidency: Law and Judgment Inside the Bush Administration,* brilliant. He agreed with Goldsmith that the torture memos were both unconstitutional and unnecessary. He testified that no presidential signing statement could override Congress's declaration that the nation's military may not engage in practices declared to be torture. Among other agreeable positions, he supported the return to the practice of limiting the number of Justice Department and White House employees authorized to communicate with each other, tolling a disorderly practice that allowed lower-level operatives to bypass their chiefs and network their ideologies.

While promising to be an attorney general for the people, as distinct from the president's lawyer, he stiff-armed Congress with an implied limitation on the legislature's ability to extract information from the executive through enforcement of contempt citations. He said the Justice Department might well decide against bringing misdemeanor contempt charges, as seemingly required by statute,[19] if it appeared that the balking official relied in good faith on higher executive authority that withholding the information was legal. Such contempt proceedings have been rare in recent years, yet the assertion of their futility was a depressing signal for cooperation between the branches. It echoed the Justice Department's advance notice to Congress not only that executive privilege would be strongly asserted in resisting White House testimony and documents concerning the firing of United States attorneys, but also that Congress could not constitutionally compel the Justice Department to enforce the criminal law to gain compliance.[20] Principal legal authority for this position comes from a 1984 Office of Legal Counsel opinion[21] supporting the department's refusal to file charges against officials involved in the Environmental Protection Agency (EPA) scandal over administration of the Superfund to clean up industrial waste sites. That opinion was signed by Theodore B. Olson, the assistant attorney general, who soon thereafter was investigated by an independent counsel in the EPA case that led to the *Morrison* v. *Olson* decision rejecting the unitary executive claims of constitutional power to ignore congressional regulation (discussed in Chapter 4).

Though not unprecedented, the Justice Department's stance, which could exalt executive privilege claims above Congress's right to information without a fight, was a classic unitary executive position. "The president has pretty much absolute power in this area," David Rivkin, a unitary executive advocate and former Bush administration lawyer, said.[22]

In confirming Mukasey without a confrontation on this issue, the Senate may have squandered the opportunity simply to withhold its stamp of approval until the White House produced the evidence. Congress could try other approaches, including one that has long been recommended, to give both chambers civil enforcement authority, scrapping the inappropriate criminal route. Or Congress could invoke its own authority, long in disuse, to conduct its own contempt proceedings. An energetic, imaginative Congress could find effective ways to overcome the intransigence of the unitary executive.

As for torture issues, Mukasey agreed broadly with Jack Goldsmith, the reluctant reviser of memos based on presidential omnipotence. He based his hesitation to pronounce on the legality of waterboarding in large part on the same concern Goldsmith had expressed. He found waterboarding, an ancient system of smothering that could drown the detainee if maintained, personally "repugnant."[23] But to declare it torture officially could subject its practitioners—and their superiors—to criminal liability, even the death penalty, for deeds deemed legal by previous official legal opinions, however erroneous they may have been.

This issue and others foretold for Mukasey many a rendezvous with his own legal reasoning and, where his opinion differed from that of Dick Cheney and David Addington, many a White House confrontation. Some senators who voted for Mukasey with mixed feelings hinted that they knew his personal legal views and expected him to disagree fundamentally with the White House. Their call for him to stand independent of his president could have been mere wishful thinking, but there was strong basis to hope that, unlike Alberto Gonzales, he would start by using his own mind rather than meekly acquiescing in the programs of the most devout unitarians. Although Mukasey might agree with many White House positions, it is hard to imagine any White House official addressing him in disgust, as Goldsmith said Addington once addressed him, "If you rule that way, the blood of the hundred thousand people who die in the next attack will be on your hands."[24]

Did the Senate once again surrender too meekly to a determined executive? Many Democrats thought so. Others excused the vote to affirm on the nominee's high reputation in the bar, his strong intellect, his pledge to restore order to the demoralized department, and above all, the president's threat to send up no other nominee, leaving the department to run on ideology. If shown powerless to have his choice confirmed, Bush turned that weakness into a kind of strength, threatening passively not to show up for this fight during his dying second term, leaving the Senate just as helpless as he. As Yogi Berra opined, "If the fans won't show up, we can't stop them."

The confirmation vote was decided by half a dozen Democrats in an otherwise party-partisan vote. It was another contemporary example of how polarized politics has become, how rare it is for legislators to vote the interest of Congress as an institution rather than hew to a party line.

The unitarians have lost and won of late. Their theory, always based on a loose construction of gossamer historical evidence, has gone down the drain, but they can cheer on their unitary president's rulemaking and even his legislative victories. The true believers may never surrender their seats in the cheering section, which means they will persist in animating and rationalizing the imperiousness of the executive. An excellent example arose from the ashes of Alberto Gonzales's resignation, in the form of an opinion article incanting "There Is Only One Executive," advising the next attorney general to resist congressional assault on the power of the presidency. Instead of berating the disgraced attorney general for squandering exective prestige and power, the writers called the issues of surveillance, Guantanamo, signing statements, and the U.S. attorney dismissals part of "the anti-Gonzales crusade."[25]

That philosophy, embodied in all branches of the unitary executive theory—tight bureaucratic control domestically and expanding power to launch wars and stiff-arm Congress—in turn helps fuel a unilateral approach to world affairs. This is of a piece with the claim of running all of our government with all the powers of an imperial chief, whose only interaction with the rest of government is dominance. Americans must seek a strong, energetic executive—but one who places a higher value on interdependence, reciprocity, and statesmanship.

Notes

1. Introduction

1. *Morrison* v. *Olson*, 487 U.S. 654 (1988).

2. Alito's speeches to the Federalist Society are cited in prepared testimony by Laurence Tribe, Confirmation Hearing on the Nomination of Samuel A. Alito, Jr., to be an associate justice of the United States, Senate Committee on the Judiciary, January 9–13, 2006, pp. 1498–1518.

2. The Framers

1. Ron Chernow, *Alexander Hamilton* (New York: Penguin Press, 2004), pp. 231–35, 241.

2. *The Federalist* No. 70 (Hamilton).

3. Terry Eastland, *Energy in the Executive* (New York: The Free Press, 1993). Eastland, public affairs officer for the Justice Department under Edwin Meese, does not use the term *unitary executive* in his book.

4. *The Federalist* No. 47 (Madison).

5. Louis Fisher, *Constitutional Conflicts Between Congress and the President*, 5th ed., rev. (Lawrence: University of Kansas Press, 2007), p. 50.

6. Potter Stewart, "Or of the Press," *Hastings Law Journal* 50 (1999): 710 (speech delivered November 2, 1974).

3. Jackson, Lincoln, Johnson, Roosevelt, Truman

1. Stephen Breyer, "For Their Own Good: The Cherokees, the Supreme Court, and the Early History of American Conscience," *New Republic*, August 7, 2000 (from speech delivered to the Supreme Court Historical Society in June 2000).

2. Louis Fisher, *Constitutional Conflicts Between Congress and the President*, 5th ed., rev. (Lawrence: University Press of Kansas, 2007) pp. 53–56.

3. William H. Rehnquist, *All the Laws But One: Civil Liberties in Wartime* (New York: Vintage Books, 2000), chapters 2–7; Daniel Farber, *Lincoln's Constitution* (Chicago: University of Chicago Press, 2003).

4. Lawrence Lessig and Cass R. Sunstein, "The President and the Administration," *Columbia Law Review* 94, no. 1 (January 1994): 78–84.

5. *Humphrey's Executor v. United States*, 295 U.S. 602 (1935).

6. *Youngstown Sheet & Tube Co. v. Sawyer*, 343 U.S. 579 (1952).

7. *Youngstown* at 612–613 (Frankfurter, concurring).

8. *Youngstown* at 634 (Jackson, concurring).

4. THE PRESIDENTIALISTS, DOMESTIC

1. Morton Rosenberg, "Congress's Prerogative Over Agencies and the Executive Branch: The Reagan Era in Retrospect," *George Washington Law Review* 57 (1989): 627; Robert Pear, "Bush Directive Increases Sway on Regulation," *New York Times*, January 31, 2007; Elena Kagan, "Presidential Administration," *Harvard Law Review* 114 (2001): 2245; Peter L. Strauss, "The Place of Agencies in Government," *Columbia Law Review* 84 (1984): 573.

2. Jeffrey Rosen, "Power of One," *New Republic,* July 24, 2006.

3. See, e.g., T. Kenneth Cribb, "Conservatism and the American Academy: Prospects for the 1990s," *Intercollegiate Review* (Spring 1990); Lee Edwards, *Educating for Liberty* (Washington, D.C.: Regnery Publishing, 2004), chapter 6, "The Rising Right"; Sidney Blumenthal, *The Rise of the Counter-Establishment: From Conservative Ideology to Political Power* (New York: Crown, 1986); Robert Huberty, "Cultural Wellspring of the Conservative Movement," *Human Events*, February 29, 2004.

4. *Using and Misusing Legislative History: A Re-Evaluation of the Status of Legislative History in Statutory Interpretation*, U.S. Department of Justice, Office of Legal Policy, Report to the Attorney General (1989).

5. *The Constitution in the Year 2000: Choices Ahead in Constitutional Interpretation*, U.S. Department of Justice, Office of Legal Policy, Report to the Attorney General (1988).

6. *Economic Liberties Protected by the Constitution*, U.S. Department of Justice, Office of Legal Policy, Report to the Attorney General (1988).

7. *McCulloch v. Maryland*, 17 U.S. 316 (1816); *On Federalism*, U.S. Department of Justice, Office of Legal Policy, Report to the Attorney General (1986). For a commentary, see "Past Federalists and Present Purists," Editorial, *New York Times,* November 15, 1986.

8. *INS* v. *Chadha*, 462 U.S. 919 (1983).

9. Neil Kinkopf, *Index of Presidential Signing Statements: 2001–2007,* American Constitution Society (August 2007).

10. Philip Hager, "Meese Attacks Supreme Court Religion Rulings: Scores Reaffirmation of Governmental Neutrality," *Los Angeles Times,* July 10, 1985.

11. Al Kamen, "Stevens Rebuts Meese Criticism of High Court," *Washington Post,* October 26, 1985.

12. Edwin Meese III, Remarks to Federalist Society 25th annual convention, November 15, 2007 (transcribed from C-Span by author).

13. Arthur J. Goldberg and Alan M. Dershowitz, "Declaring the Death Penalty Unconstitutional," *Harvard Law Review* 83 (1970): 1773.

14. The speech was republished in Edwin Meese, "The Law of the Constitution," *Tulane University Law Review* 61 (1987): 983.

15. Edwin Meese, "Perspective on the Authoritativeness of Supreme Court Decision: The Law of the Constitution," *Tulane Law Review* 61 (1987): 979.

16. Memo from Samuel A. Alito, Jr., Deputy Assistant Attorney General, Office of Legal Counsel, to the Litigation Strategy Working Group, February 5, 1986 (reproduced from the holdings of the National Archives and Records Administration, Record Group 60, Department of Justice Files of Stephen Galebach, 1985–1987, Accession 060-89-269, Box 6, Folder: SG/Litigation Strategy Working Group).

17. 478 U.S. 714 (1986).

18. Charles Fried, *Order and Law* (New York: Oxford University Press, 1991), pp. 159–160.

19. Bernard Schwartz, "An Administrative Law 'Might Have Been'— Chief Justice Burger's *Bowsher* v. *Synar* Draft," *Administrative Law Review* 42 (1990): 233.

20. *Report of the Congressional Committees Investigating the Iran-Contra Affair, with Supplemental, Minority, and Additional Views,* U.S. Senate Report No. 100-216, House of Representatives Report No. 100-433 (1987), p. 463.

21. Office of Watergate Special Prosecution Force Regulation, 38 Fed. Reg. 4,688 (1973).

22. *United States* v. *Nixon,* 418 U.S. 683 (1974).

23. *in re Sealed Case,* 838 F.2d 476 (1988).

24. *Morrison* v. *Olson,* 487 U.S. 654 (1988).

25. Jay S. Bybee and Tuan N. Samahon, "William Rehnquist, the Separation of Powers and the Riddle of the Sphinx," *Stanford Law Review* 58 (2006): 1735.

26. Ibid., p. 1744, quoting Memorandum from William H. Rehnquist, Assistant Attorney General, Office of Legal Counsel, to the Honorable Edward

L. Morgan, Deputy Counsel to the President, Re: Presidential Authority to Impound Funds Appropriated for Assistance to Federally Impacted Schools (December 1, 1969), reprinted in *Executive Impoundment of Appropriated Funds: Hearings Before the Subcommittee on Separation of Powers of the Senate Committee on the Judiciary,* 92d Cong., 279–91 (1971).

27. See Bernard Schwartz, "Curiouser and Curiouser: The Supreme Court's Separation of Powers Wonderland," *Notre Dame Law Review* 65 (1990): 587.

28. Ibid.

29. Philip Shenon, "Special Prosecutor Drops E.P.A. Case without Indictment," *New York Times,* August 27, 1988.

30. Ronald J. Ostrow, "Independent Counsel Explains Why She Didn't Prosecute Figure in '83 EPA Probe," *Los Angeles Times,* March 21, 1989.

31. Fried, *Order and Law,* p. 160.

32. Ibid., p. 165.

33. Ibid., p.168.

34. *Mistretta* v. *United States,* 488 U.S. 361 (1989).

35. Charles Fried, *Order and Law,* p. 170.

5. The Presidentialists, Domestic and Global

1. The four articles are Steven G. Calabresi and Christopher S. Yoo, "The Unitary Executive During the First Half-Century," *Case Western Reserve Law Review* 47 (1997): 1451; Steven G. Calabresi and Christopher S. Yoo, "The Unitary Executive During the Second Half-Century," *Harvard Journal of Law and Public Policy* 26 (2003): 667; Christopher S. Yoo, Steven G. Calabresi, and Laurence D. Nee, "The Unitary Executive During the Third Half-Century, 1889–1945," *Notre Dame Law Review* 80 (2004): 1; and Christopher S. Yoo, Steven G. Calabresi, and Anthony J. Colangelo, "The Unitary Executive in the Modern Era, 1945–2004," *Iowa Law Review* 90 (January 2005): 601.

2. Yoo et al., "The Unitary Executive in the Modern Era, 1945–2004," pp. 729–31.

3. Charlie Savage, *Takeover: The Return of the Imperial Presidency and the Subversion of American Democracy* (New York: Little, Brown, 2007), pp. 50–57; Frederick A. O. Schwarz and Aziz Z. Huq, *Unchecked and Unbalanced: Presidential Power in a Time of Terror* (New York: The New Press, 2007), p.1; Stephen F. Hayes, *Cheney: The Untold Story of*

America's Most Powerful and Controversial Vice President (New York: Harper Collins, 2007) p. 490.

4. *Report of the Congressional Committees Investigating the Iran-Contra Affair, with Supplemental, Minority and Additional Views,* U.S. Senate Report No. 100-216, House of Representatives Report No. 100-433 (1987), p. 463.

5. From a Nixon-Frost interview that aired May 17, 1977, excerpt printed in *New York Times,* May 20, 1977.

6. THE PRESIDENTIALISTS, GLOBAL

1. John C. Yoo, "The Continuation of Politics by Other Means: The Original Understanding of War Powers," *California Law Review* 84, no. 2 (1996): 167, reproduced in John C. Yoo, *The Powers of War and Peace: The Constitution and Foreign Affairs after 9/11* (Chicago: University of Chicago Press, 2005).

2. James Madison, *The Writings of James Madison,* vol. 6, Gaillard Hunt, ed. (1906), p. 148 (emphasis in original), cited in Louis Fisher, "Lost Constitutional Moorings: Recovering the War Power," *Indiana Law Journal* 81 (2005): 1205.

3. Paul M. Barrett, "Opinion Maker—A Young Lawyer Helps Chart Shift in Foreign Policy," *Wall Street Journal,* September 12, 2005.

4. Charlie Savage, *Takeover: The Return of the Imperial Presidency and the Subversion of American Democracy* (New York: Little, Brown, 2007), pp. 79–80.

5. Authorization for Use of Military Force, 115 Statt. 224, Public Law 107-40, 107th Congress (September 18, 2001): "Whereas, the President has authority under the Constitution to take action to deter and prevent acts of international terrorism against the United States: Now, therefore, be it Resolved. . . . That the President is authorized to use all necessary and appropriate force against those nations, organizations, or persons he determines planned, authorized, committed, or harbored such organizations or persons."

6. John C. Yoo, Deputy Assistant Attorney General, to Timothy Flanigan, Deputy Counsel to the President, September 25, 2001, "The President's Constitutional Authority to Conduct Military Operations Against Terrorists and Nations Supporting Them," available in *The Torture Papers,* ed. Karen J. Greenberg and Joshua L. Dratal (New York: Cambridge University Press, 2005), p. 3.

7. Ibid.

8. Ibid., p. 8.

9. Ibid., p. 7.

10. Ibid. p. 5, citing Yoo, "The Continuation of Politics by Other Means."

11. Fisher, "Lost Constitutional Moorings," p. 1241.

12. John C. Yoo and Patrick Philbin to Haynes re Possible Habeas Jurisdiction over Aliens Held in Guantanamo Bay, Cuba, December 28, 2001, available in *The Torture Papers,* pp. 29–37.

13. This memo, dated August 1, 2002, is available in *The Torture Papers,* pp. 172–217.

14. John Yoo, *War by Other Means: An Insider's Accout of the War on Terror* (New York: Atlantic Monthly Press, 2006).

15. *Hamdi* v. *Rumsfeld,* 542 U.S. 507 (2004).

16. *Rasul* v. *Bush,* 542 U.S. 466 (2004).

17. *Hamdan* v. *Rumsfeld,* 165 L.Ed.2d 723 (June 29, 2006).

18. Adam Liptak, "The Court Enters the War, Loudly," *New York Times,* July 2, 2006.

19. John C. Yoo, "Congress to Courts: 'Get Out of the War on Terror,'" *Wall Street Journal,* October 19, 2006, p. A18.

20. *Hamdan,154* L.Ed. 2d at 780 (Breyer, joined by Kennnedy, Souter, and Ginsburg, concurring).

7. THE WILL AND PLEASURE OF THE PRESIDENT

1. Preserving Prosecutorial Independence, Senate Judiciary Committee hearing, May 15, 2007.

2. Alberto Gonzales, testimony, Senate Judiciary Committee, April 19, 2007.

3. *Morrison* v. *Olson,* 487 U.S. 654, 676–677 ("Lower courts have also upheld judicial appointments of United States Attorneys, see *United States* v. *Solomon,* 216 F. Supp. 835 (SDNY 1963), and Congress itself has vested the power to make these interim appointments in the district courts, see 28 U. S. C. § 546(d) (1982 ed., Supp. V).").

4. For floor discussion on House passage of H.R. 580, see *Congressional Record* (March 26, 2007), pp. H3035-3041.

5. Charlie Savage, "In Terror War's Name, Public Loses Information," *Boston Globe,* April 24, 2005.

6. Charlie Savage, *Takeover: The Return of the Imperial Presidency and the Subversion of American Democracy* (New York: Little, Brown, 2007), p. 97.

7. Robert Pear, "Inquiry Confirms Top Medicare Official Threatened Actuary Over Cost of Drug Benefits," *New York Times*, July 7, 2004; "The Foster Affair," Editorial, *New York Times*, July 13, 2004.

8. *Reynolds v. United States*, 346 U.S. 826 (1953). A full account of the case and its aftermath is in Louis Fisher, *In the Name of National Security* (Lawrence: University of Kansas Press, 2006).

9. *Cheney v. U.S. District Court*, 542 U.S. 367 (2004) and related cases.

10. See Linda Greenhouse, "Justices Turn Aside Case of Man Accusing C.I.A. of Torture," *New York Times*, October 10, 2007, p. A20.

8. SIGNING STATEMENTS

1. President's Statement on Signing of H.R. 2863, the "Department of Defense, Emergency Supplemental Appropriations to Address Hurricanes in the Gulf of Mexico, and Pandemic Influenza Act, 2006," *Weekly Compilation of Presidential Documents* 41 (December 30, 2005): 1918.

2. U.S. Congress, Senate Judiciary Committee, Confirmation Hearing on the Nomination of Samuel A. Alito, Jr. to be an Associate Justice of the Supreme Court of the United States, 109th Congress 2d Session, January 9–13, 2006.

3. Ibid., p. 483.

4. Ibid., pp. 713, 1498 (Fried live and prepared testimony); pp. 714, 1498 (Tribe live and prepared testimony).

5. American Bar Association Task Force on Presidential Signing Statements and the Separation of Powers Doctrine, August 2006.

6. Walter Dellinger, "A Slip of the Pen," *New York Times*, July 31, 2006. See also Dellinger memos to Bernard N. Nussbaum, Counsel to the President, November 3, 1993, and to Abner J. Mikva, Counsel to the President, November 2, 1994.

7. Prepared testimony of Michelle E. Boardman, Deputy Assistant Attorney General, Department of Justice, before Senate Judiciary Committee, June 27, 2006.

8. U.S. Department of Justice, Office of the Inspector General, *A Review of the Federal Bureau of Investigation's Use of National Security Letters* (March 2007); John Solomon and Barton Gellman, "Frequent Errors in FBI's Secret Records Requests," *Washington Post,* March 9, 2007; John Solomon, "FBI Issues New Rules for Getting Phone Records," *Washington Post,* March 20, 2007.

9. *Hamdan* v. *Rumsfeld*, 165 L.Ed. 2d 723, 799 (June 29, 2006, Scalia, J., dissenting).

10. *Buckley* v. *Valeo*, 424 U.S. 1, 132 (1976).

11. "Statement on Signing the Civil Rights Act of 1991," *Weekly Compilation of Presidential Documents* 27 (November 21, 1991): 1702. "Remarks on Signing the Civil Rights Act of 1991," *Published Papers* 2 (November 21, 1991): 1503. Described in "Context-Sensitive Deference to Presidential Signing Statements," *Harvard Law Review* 120 (2006): 615–18; Andrew Rosenthal, "Reaffirming Commitment, Bush Signs Rights Bill," *New York Times*, November 22, 1991, p. 1; "Thumbing His Nose at Congress; President Bush Signs–and Undermines–the Rights Bill," Editorial, *New York Times*, November 22, 1991, p. A30.

12. Rosenthal, "Reaffirming Commitment, Bush Signs Rights Bill."

13. Jonathan Weisman, "Signing Statements' Study Finds Administration Has Ignored Laws," *Washington Post*, June 19, 2007, p. A4.

14. Testimony of Deputy Assistant Attorney General Michelle E. Boardman, Senate Judiciary Committee, June 27, 2006.

15. Memo from Samuel A. Alito, Jr., Deputy Assistant Attorney General, Office of Legal Counsel, to the Litigation Strategy Working Group, February 5, 1986 (reproduced from the holdings of the National Archives and Records Administration, Record Group 60, Department of Justice Files of Stephen Galebach, 1985–1987, Accession 060-89-269, Box 6, Folder: SG/Litigation Strategy Working Group).

9. Theory and Consequence

1. *Youngstown Sheet & Tube Co.* v. *Sawyer*, 343 U.S. 579, 635 (1952), Jackson, J., concurring.

2. For a comprehensive description of the pre-*Hamdan* imbalance, see Frederick A. O. Schwarz and Aziz Z. Huq, *Unchecked and Unbalanced* (New York: The New Press, 2007).

3. Jack Goldsmith, *The Terror Presidency: Law and Judgment inside the Bush Administration* (New York: W. W. Norton, 2007), p. 89.

4. Ibid., pp. 148–49.

5. Goldsmith, *The Terror Presidency*, p. 145.

6. Ibid., p. 165.

7. Ibid., p. 129.

8. Scott Shane, David Johnston, and James Risen, "Secret U.S. Endorsement of Severe Interrogations," *New York Times,* October 4, 2007, p. A1.

9. See, e.g., Adam Nagourney and Marc Santora, "Romney and Giuliani Spar as New Guy Looks On," *New York Times,* October 10, 2007.

10. Jim Rutenberg, "Clinton Plans to Consider Giving Up Some Powers," *New York Times,* October 24, 2007.

11. *Boumediene* v. *Bush,* No. 06-1195, *Al Odah* v. *United States,* cert. granted June 29, 2007.

12. John C. Yoo, "The Continuation of Politics by Other Means: The Original Understanding of War Powers," *California Law Review* 84, no. 2 (March 1996): 170, reproduced in John C. Yoo, *The Powers of War and Peace: The Constitution and Foreign Affairs after 9/11* (Chicago: University of Chicago Press, 2005).

13. For example, *Lopez* v. *United States,* 514 U.S. 549 (1995).

14. For example, *City of Boerne* v. *Flores,* 521 U.S. 507 (1997).

15. 531 U.S. 98 (2000).

16. *Bush* v. *Gore,* 531 U.S. 1046-7 (Scalia, J., concurring in the issuance of stay), December 9, 2000.

17. See Thomas E. Mann and Norman J. Ornstein, *The Broken Branch: How Congress Is Failing America and How to Get It Back on Track* (New York: Oxford University Press, 2006).

18. Carl Hulse, "Democrats Move to Block Bush Appointments," *New York Times,* November 21, 2007.

19. Title 2, Section 192 of the United States Code provides that willful refusal to produce documents in response to a congressional subpoena is a misdemeanor. Section 194 provides that if such a failure is reported to either house of Congress it "shall" be certified to the "appropriate United States attorney whose duty it shall be to bring the matter before the grand jury for its action."

20. Dan Eggen and Amy Goldstein, "Broader Privilege Claimed in Firings," *Washington Post,* July 20, 2007, p. A1.

21. 8 U.S. Op. Office of Legal Counsel 101 (1984).

22. Peter Baker, "White House Will Deny New Request in Attorneys Probe; Bush to Defy Congress, Sources Say," *Washington Post,* July 8, 2007, p. A3.

23. Scott Shane, "Nominee Describes Harsh Interrogation as Repugnant," *New York Times,* October 31, 2007.

24. Goldsmith, *The Terror Presidency,* p. 71

25. David B. Rivkin, Jr., and Lee A. Casey, "There Is Only One Executive," *Wall Street Journal,* August 28, 2007.

INDEX

Abu Ghraib, 39, 49

Addington, David, 31, 37, 56, 61

Alito, Samuel A., Jr., 2, 20–21, 50, 51, 54, 59

American Bar Association, 51

Armed Services Committee, 42

Articles of Confederation, 38

Ashcroft, John, 44, 45, 47

Authorization for the Use of Military Force, 39

Balanced Budget and Emergency Deficit Control Act of 1985, 21

Bill of Rights, 9, 20

Black, Hugo, 15

Boardman, Michelle E., 51, 52

Bolton, John, 28

Bork, Robert H., 23, 36, 46

Boston Globe, 37, 51

Bowsher, Charles A., 21

Bowsher v. *Synar* (1986), 21

Bradbury, Steven, 57

Brandeis, Louis D., 14

Brennan, William J., Jr., 20

Breyer, Stephen, 41

Burger, Warren, 22

Bush, George H.W., 53

Bush, George W.: and federal prosecutor firings, 43; presidential signing statements by, 19, 20,
49, 51; and secrecy, 44; and unitary executive, 1–2, 3, 31–32; and war on terror, 37

Bush v. *Gore* (2000), 58

Bybee, Jay, 26, 38, 39

Calabresi, Steven G.: on Bush administration, 32, 33, 34; and Federalist Society, 36; on unitary executive, 18, 31, 52

Campaign Reform Act of 1974, 53

Capital punishment, 20

Card, Andrew, 45

Central Intelligence Agency (CIA), 33

Chadha, Jagdish Rai, 19

Chadha; Immigration and Naturalization Service v. (1983), 19

Cheney, Dick: and Iran-contra scandal, 23, 33; and Mukasey, 61; and secrecy, 44; and unitary executive, 1–2; and war on terror, 31, 32, 37

Cherokee treaty, 13

Civil enforcement authority, 61

Civil Rights Act of 1964, 53

Civil Rights Restoration Act of 1991, 53

Clinton, Bill, 51, 58

Clinton, Hillary, 57

Comey, James, 45, 47

Congress: and independent counsels, 23; powers of, 19; reform of, 59
Constitution: Article I, 10–11, 58; Article II, 11, 13, 24, 26, 33, 37, 55; Article III, 11; declare war clause, 35; necessary and proper clause, 11, 19; take care clause, 10, 11, 12, 33. See also specific amendments
Constitutional convention, 6, 9, 25, 35
Conyers, John, Jr., 54
Cox, Archibald, 23
Cribb, T. Kenneth, 18
Cruel and unusual punishment, 20

Danforth, John, 54
Death penalty, 20
"Decision of 1789," 9, 10
Declaration of Independence, 6
Declare war clause, 35
Dellinger, Walter, 51
Democrats, 2, 42
Dershowitz, Alan, 20
Detainees and enemy combatants, 38, 40, 41, 42, 57
District of Columbia, U.S. Court of Appeals, 24
Dred Scott v. Sandford (1857), 14

Eastland, Terry, 20, 63n3
Eavesdropping program. See Terrorism Surveillance Program
Eighth Amendment, 20
Emancipation Proclamation, 14
Enemy combatants. See Detainees and enemy combatants
"Energy in the executive," 7, 36, 55, 63n3

Environmental Protection Agency (EPA), 60
Ethics in Government Act of 1978, 27
Executive privilege, 23, 60

Federal agencies, independence of, 21
Federal Bar Association, 21
Federal Bureau of Investigation (FBI), 33, 52
Federal Election Commission, 53
The Federalist: generally, 6–9, 36, 55; No. 37, 7; No. 47, 27; No. 70, 22; No. 71, 7
Federalist Society, 18, 31, 34, 36, 58
Federal prosecutors, 25–26, 43, 45, 58, 60
Federal Trade Commission Act of 1914, 15
Feinstein, Dianne, 45, 46
Fine, Glen A., 52
Fisher, Louis, 38, 63n5, 67n2, 67n11, 68n8
Fitzgerald, Patrick, 47, 48
Flanigan, Tim, 37
Ford, Gerald, 53
Foreign Intelligence Surveillance Act (FISA, 1978), 43, 44
Fourteenth Amendment, 20, 58
Fourth Amendment, 44
Framers, 5–11, 25, 26–27
Frankfurter, Felix, 15
Freedom of Information Act of 1966, 46
Fried, Charles, 22, 25, 27, 28, 29, 50
Frost, David, 33
Geneva Conventions, 38, 40, 42, 57
George III, 6, 35
Ginsburg, Ruth Bader, 25

Goldberg, Arthur J., 20
Goldsmith, Jack, 56–57, 59–60, 61
Gonzales, Alberto, 38, 43, 45, 61, 62
Government Accountability Office, 54
Governors, 20
Graham, Lindsey, 42
Gramm-Rudman-Hollings Act of 1985, 21, 53
Greenhouse, Linda, 69n10
Guantanamo Bay, 38, 39, 40, 41. *See also* Detainees and enemy combatants

Habeas corpus, 38, 40, 41, 42, 57, 58
Hamdan v. *Rumsfeld* (2006), 40, 41, 42, 53, 55, 57, 59
Hamdi, Yaser Esa, 39
Hamdi v. *Rumsfeld* (2004), 32, 39
Hamilton, Alexander, 5, 6, 7, 22, 25, 36, 55
Hatch, Orrin, 36
Haynes, William, 38
Holmes, Oliver Wendell, 14
Humphrey, William E., 15
Humphrey's Executor v. *United States* (1935), 15
Huq, Aziz, 66n3, 70n2
Immigration and Naturalization Service v. *Chadha* (1983), 19
Impeachment: of Johnson, 14; of Nixon, 33
Impoundment, 26, 65n25
Independent Counsel Act of 1978, 23, 36
Independent counsels, 23, 24, 46, 47, 60
Inherent powers: and Bush, 2, 20, 31–32; and Cheney, 23; and Truman,

15; war and foreign affairs, 5–6, 37–38, 50
Interrogation, 38, 39
Interstate Commerce Commission, 18
Iran-contra scandal, 23, 33

Jackson, Andrew, 13–16, 18
Jackson, Robert H., 15–16, 40, 56
Jaworsky, Leon, 23
Jay, John, 7
Johnson, Andrew, 14, 18
Judicial Conference of the United States, 28

Kennedy, Edward, 28
Kmiec, Douglas, 28
Korean War, 15, 37
Korea Times and Yoo, 37

Legislative veto, 19, 20, 52
Libby, I. Lewis (Scooter), 47–48
Lincoln, Abraham, 14, 18
Liptak, Adam, 68n18

Madison, James, 6, 7–8, 10, 25, 26–27, 36
Markman, Steven J., 18
Marshall, John, 19, 26
Massachusetts constitution, 8–9
Matthews, Chris, 57
McCain, John, 42, 49, 50, 52
McCulloch v. *Maryland* (1816), 64n7
Meese, Edwin, III: as Attorney General, 18–22; and independent counsels, 23, 24; and unitary executive, 5, 17, 32, 36
Military Commission Act of 2006, 41, 42, 58

Military commission system, 40, 41, 57
Military force, 38, 39
Mistretta v. *United States* (1989), 66n32
Monarchy, 35
Monroe, James, 51
Montesquieu, Baron de, 8
Morrison, Alexia, 25, 26
Morrison v. *Olson* (1988): and Meese, 23; and Olson, 60; Scalia on, 29, 32; and unitary executive, 25, 27, 46, 55
Mueller, Robert S., III, 52
Mukasey, Michael, 59–61
Myers, Frank, 14
Myers v. *United States* (1926), 14

National Security Letters, 52
Necessary and proper clause, 11, 19
New Deal, 3, 18, 32
New York Times 64n1, 64n7, 66n27, 68n18, 69n10, 69n6, 69n11, 70n10; on torture memo, 57
Nixon, Richard M., 23, 26, 33
Nixon; United States v. (1974), 65n21

O'Connor, Sandra Day, 22, 39
Office of Legal Counsel, 24, 26, 36, 51, 56, 57, 60
Office of Managment and Budget (OMB), 17
Olson, Theodore B., 24, 25, 27, 41

Pardon power, 44, 48
Patriot Act Reauthorization of 2005, 45, 52
Philbin, Patrick, 38
Plame, Valerie, 47–48

Plural executive, 25
Preemptive military action, 38
Presidential intent, 21
Presidentialists: combination, 31–34; domestic, 17–29; global, 35–42
Public Records Preservation Act of 1988, 46

Rasul v. *Bush* (2004), 40
Reagan, Ronald, 2–3, 21–22, 51, 53
Rehnquist, William, 25, 26, 46
Removal powers, 10, 12, 14–15, 21, 23, 33
Republicans, 2, 22–23
Reynolds; United States v. (1953), 47
Rivkin, David, 60
Roberts, John G., 59
Roosevelt, Franklin D., 14–15, 18, 52

Saturday Night Massacre, 23
Savage, Charlie, 37, 51, 66n3, 57n4, 68n5, 68n6
Scalia, Antonin, 26, 27, 29, 32, 53, 59
Schmults, Edward C., 24
Schwartz, Bernard, 22
Schwarz, Frederick A. O., 66n3, 70n2
Secrecy, 44, 46
Sentencing Commission, 28, 29
Sentencing Reform Act of 1984, 28
Separation of powers, 25, 28, 36, 48
September 11, 2001, terrorist attacks, 3, 37, 38
Signing statements, 19, 49–54
Silberman, Laurence H., 25, 36
Smith, William French, 18
Souter, David, 40
Specter, Arlen, 42, 46, 51, 52

"Standards of Conduct for Interrogation under 18 U.S.C. §§2340-2340A," 38

State secrets privilege, 46–47

Steel Seizure Case. *See Youngstown Sheet & Tube Co. v. Sawyer*

Stevens, John Paul, 20

Stewart, Potter, 11

Superfund, 24, 60

Supreme Court: on detainees and enemy combatants, 39; and habeas corpus, 58; and independent counsels, 23, 25; and removal powers, 14, 15, 21; on Sentencing Commission, 29; on state secrets privilege, 47; on unitary executive, 2, 3, 55

Surveillance program, domestic. *See* Terrorism Surveillance Program

Sutherland, Arthur, 15

Taft, William Howard, 10, 14, 15

Taft-Hartley Act of 1947, 15

Take care clause, 10, 11, 12, 33

Taliban detainees, 38

Tenure of Office Act of 1867, 14

Terrorism. *See* September 11, 2001 terrorist attacks; War on terror

Terrorism Surveillance Program, 43, 44, 45

The Terror Presidency: Law and Judgment Inside the Bush Administration (Goldsmith), 59–60

Thomas, Clarence, 36, 39, 59

Thornburgh, Dick, 28

Title VII of Civil Rights Act, 53

Torture, 2, 3, 38–39, 49–50, 52, 61

Torture memo, 3, 26, 38, 39, 41, 56–57, 67n6

Tribe, Laurence H., 50–51

Truman, Harry S., 15, 37

Uniform Code of Military Justice, 40, 42

Unitarians, 17

Unitary executive, 1–4, 5–7, 18, 22, 25–27, 39, 50, 55

United States v. *See name of opposing party*

United States Attorneys, 25–26, 43, 45, 58, 60

United States Court of Appeals for the District of Columbia, 24, 25

United States Sentencing Commission, 28, 29

Valerie Plame leak case, 47–48

Van Devanter, Willis, 14

Wall Street Journal, 67n3, 68n19, 71n18

Walsh, Lawrence E., 24

Warner, John, 41–42

War on terror, 3, 31–32, 37

Washington Post, 70n13

Waterboarding, 61

West Publishing Company, 21

White House travel office staff, 58

Williams, Stephen F., 25

Wilson, Woodrow, 14

Wiretapping program. *See* Terrorism Surveillance Program

Yoo, John, 31–41, 50, 56, 57

Youngstown Sheet & Tube Co. v. Sawyer (1952), 15, 16, 32, 40, 56, 57

ABOUT THE AUTHOR

JOHN P. MACKENZIE was a reporter for the *Washington Post* (1956–77), covering the Supreme Court for a decade, and a *New York Times* editorial writer (1977–97). He has been a visiting professor of law and a visiting scholar at NYU School of Law. He is the author of *The Appearance of Justice* (Scribners, 1974), which concerns the ethical lapses of judges and justices. He also is the author of "Life after Sunset," about current Justice Department regulations for picking outside independent counsel, for the *Widener Law Symposium Journal* (2000) and he contributed a chapter, "Equal Protection for One Lucky Guy," about the *Bush* v. *Gore* decision, to *The Rehnquist Court*, Herman Schwartz, ed. (Hill & Wang, 2002).